English Across the World

Akihiko Sato
Richard Heselton

Student ID No. : _____

Name : _____

photographs by

iStockphoto

photolibrary

Getty Images

音声ファイルのダウンロード／ストリーミング

CDマーク表示がある箇所は、音声を弊社HPより無料でダウンロード／ストリーミングすることができます。下記URL の書籍詳細ページに音声ダウンロードアイコンがございますのでそちらから自習用音声としてご活用ください。

https://www.seibido.co.jp/ad707

English Across the World

Copyright © 2025 by Akihiko Sato

All rights reserved for Japan.
No part of this book may be reproduced in any form
without permission from Seibido Co., Ltd.

はしがき

English Across the World（世界をめぐる発信型総合英語）は、日本に住む英語学習者が海外の若者の生活に触れ、感情移入しながら学べる新しいタイプの総合教材です。世界の国々に関する基本情報や文化について理解しながら、英語の「聴く・話す・読む・書く」技能がバランスよく伸ばせます。日本の英語教育に即し、一般的なアメリカ英語を基準としており、レベル設定は CEFR A1-A2 に合わせています。

各ユニットのインプットとして、ターゲットとなる「文法」を明瞭な解説と親しみやすい例文により学びます。一貫して文法が身につくタスクを提供しており、「トリビア」では世界各国の興味深い事実を通じて読解力を養い、「会話」では現地大学生の日常生活に共感しつつ自然な英語に触れます。そして、最終タスクの「発表」を通じて英語のアウトプットに自信が持てるようになることを到達目標としています。

この刊行に際し、株式会社成美堂の佐野泰一氏には企画から編集、校正、録音に至るまで幅広くお力添えをいただき、そのおかげで本書の完成につながりました。この場を借りて深く感謝申し上げます。

2025 年 1 月

佐藤 明彦

本書の構成・使い方

各ユニットの国について理解しながらターゲットとなる「文法」を学び、「トリビア」、「会話」を経て最終タスクの「発表」につなげましょう。

国の説明

国の基本情報を読み概要を理解しましょう。巻頭の「国の基本データ」も参照し、日本との比較をしましょう。

Unit 1：イタリア	Unit 6：ニュージーランド	Unit 11：ケニア
Unit 2：マレーシア	Unit 7：タイ	Unit 12：フランス
Unit 3：イギリス	Unit 8：アメリカ	Unit 13：アイルランド
Unit 4：エジプト	Unit 9：フィンランド	Unit 14：ペルー
Unit 5：ドイツ	Unit 10：ベルギー	

Vocabulary

ユニットで使われる難しいレベルの語を確認し覚えましょう。

Word Mapping

国に関するキーワードを確認し、気になったものは調べましょう。

Target Grammar

ユニットの核となるターゲット文法を学びます。例文を理解し用法を学びましょう。

Unit 1：動詞	Unit 6：進行形	Unit 11：仮定法
Unit 2：人称代名詞・冠詞	Unit 7：比較級	Unit 12：関係代名詞
Unit 3：助動詞	Unit 8：最上級	Unit 13：接続詞
Unit 4：受動態	Unit 9：不定詞・動名詞	Unit 14：前置詞
Unit 5：現在完了	Unit 10：使役動詞	

Completing Sentences / **Word Order**

文法に関する確認問題を解き理解を深めましょう。／文法を使った整序問題を解き作文の力を養いましょう。

Reading Trivia 🔊音声あり

国に関するトリビアから興味深い豆知識を学びます。

U 1：ピザ・マルゲリータの始まり	U 6：ハカダンスのレガシー	U 11：長距離ランナーの秘密
U 2：クアラルンプールという地名	U 7：微笑みの国	U 12：ココ・シャネルの家
U 3：ザ・ビートルズのオーディション	U 8：ギフト、自由の女神	U 13：ギネスブックとビール
U 4：スフィンクスの探求	U 9：サウナと世界のつながり	U 14：インカ帝国、幻の都市
U 5：アディダスとプーマの創設者	U 10：ゴディバのロゴ	

(1) 本文を読み理解しましょう。（音声を活用したパラレルリーディングもお勧めです。）

(2) トリビアにおける多肢選択問題を解き読解力を高めましょう。

Conversation with Listening 🔊音声あり

現地の大学生の会話から役立つフレーズを学びます。（英文は一般的なアメリカ英語を基に構成されています。）

(1) 音声を聴き空所補充をしましょう。（音声を活用したパラレルリーディング、ロールプレイもお勧めです。）

(2) 会話内容における正誤問題を解き理解を深めましょう。

Presentation 🔊音声あり

現地の大学生の発表を確認し、自らの発表につなげましょう。（英文は一般的なアメリカ英語を基に構成されています。）

(1) モデルとなる発表を確認しましょう。（音声を活用したパラレルリーディングもお勧めです。）

(2) 自分の発表原稿を完成させ、ペア・グループ内で発表しましょう。空所には自分に沿った内容を記入しますが、選択肢の語句を使ってもかまいません。（内容が当てはまらなくても役割練習として取り組みましょう。）

Contents

UNIT 1

Country	Trivia	Grammar	Page
イタリア Italy	ピザ・マルゲリータの始まり The Start of Pizza Margherita	動詞 Verb	10

UNIT 2

Country	Trivia	Grammar	Page
マレーシア Malaysia	クアラルンプールという地名 The Name of Kuala Lumpur	人称代名詞・冠詞 Personal Pronoun / Article	16

UNIT 3

Country	Trivia	Grammar	Page
イギリス The UK	ザ・ビートルズのオーディション The Beatles Audition	助動詞 Auxiliary Verb	22

UNIT 4

Country	Trivia	Grammar	Page
エジプト Egypt	スフィンクスの探求 Exploring the Great Sphinx	受動態 Passive Voice	28

UNIT 5

Country	Trivia	Grammar	Page
ドイツ Germany	アディダスとプーマの創設者 Founders of Adidas and Puma	現在完了 Present Perfect	34

UNIT 6

Country	Trivia	Grammar	Page
ニュージーランド New Zealand	ハカダンスのレガシー The Haka Dance Legacy	進行形 Progressive	40

UNIT 7

Country	Trivia	Grammar	Page
タイ Thailand	微笑みの国 The Land of Smiles	比較級 Comparative	46

UNIT 8

Country	Trivia	Grammar	Page
アメリカ The USA	ギフト、自由の女神 The Gift of the Statue of Liberty	最上級 Superlative	52

UNIT 9

Country	Trivia	Grammar	Page
フィンランド Finland	サウナと世界のつながり Saunas Worldwide	不定詞・動名詞 Infinitive / Gerund	58

UNIT 10

Country	Trivia	Grammar	Page
ベルギー Belgium	ゴディバのロゴ The Logo of GODIVA	使役動詞 Causative Verb	64

UNIT 11

Country	Trivia	Grammar	Page
ケニア Kenya	長距離ランナーの秘密 The Secret of Distance Runners	仮定法 Subjunctive Mood	70

UNIT 12

Country	Trivia	Grammar	Page
フランス France	ココ・シャネルの家 The House of Coco Chanel	関係代名詞 Relative Pronoun	76

UNIT 13

Country	Trivia	Grammar	Page
アイルランド Ireland	ギネスブックとビール The Guinness Book and Beer	接続詞 Conjunction	82

UNIT 14

Country	Trivia	Grammar	Page
ペルー Peru	インカ帝国、幻の都市 The Lost City of the Incas	前置詞 Preposition	88

国の基本データ

課	参考	Unit 1	Unit 2	Unit 3	Unit 4	Unit 5	Unit 6
国	日本	イタリア	マレーシア	イギリス	エジプト	ドイツ	ニュージーラ
	Japan	Italy	Malaysia	The UK	Egypt	Germany	New Zeala
首都	Tokyo	Rome	Kuala Lumpur	London	Cairo	Berlin	Wellingto
面積	377,974㎢	302,000㎢	330,000㎢	243,000㎢	1,000,000㎢	357,000㎢	275,340
人口	124,600,000	59,000,000	35,100,000	67,300,000	111,700,000	84,800,000	5,250,00
主な言語	日本語	イタリア語	マレー語、中国語、英語	英語	アラビア語	ドイツ語	英語、マオリ語手話
通貨	円 (JPY)	ユーロ (EUR)	リンギット (MYR)	ポンド (GBP)	エジプト・ポンド (EGP)	ユーロ (EUR)	ニュージーランドル (NZD)
政治・議会	議院内閣制・二院制	共和制・二院制	立憲君主制・二院制	立憲君主制・両院制	共和制・二院制	連邦共和制・二院制	立憲君主制一院制
主な宗教	仏教、神道	キリスト教	イスラム教、仏教、キリスト教、ヒンドゥー教	キリスト教	イスラム教、キリスト教	キリスト教	キリスト教
主な産業	自動車、電子機器、化学薬品、観光	観光、機械、化学薬品、繊維	電子機器、石油・ガス、パーム油、ゴム	機械、航空機、化学薬品、石油・ガス、観光	石油・ガス、観光、農業、繊維	自動車、機械、鉄鋼、化学薬品、観光	畜産、農業木材、観光
観光名所	清水寺	コロッセオ	ペトロナス・ツインタワー	バッキンガム宮殿	ギザのピラミッド	ノイシュバンシュタイン城	ホビット村
特徴的な食品	寿司	ピザ	ロティチャナイ	フィッシュ＆チップス	ターメイヤ	ザワークラウト	キウイフル

Unit 7	Unit 8	Unit 9	Unit 10	Unit 11	Unit 12	Unit 13	Unit 14
タイ	アメリカ	フィンランド	ベルギー	ケニア	フランス	アイルランド	ペルー
Thailand	The USA	Finland	Belgium	Kenya	France	Ireland	Peru
Bangkok	Washington, D.C.	Helsinki	Brussels	Nairobi	Paris	Dublin	Lima
514,000㎢	9,833,517㎢	338,000㎢	30,528㎢	583,000㎢	549,134㎢	70,300㎢	1,290,000㎢
71,100,000	334,000,000	5,540,000	11,800,000	55,300,000	68,300,000	5,300,000	33,800,000
タイ語	英語、スペイン語	フィンランド語	オランダ語、フランス語、ドイツ語	スワヒリ語、英語	フランス語	英語、ゲール語	スペイン語
バーツ (THB)	ドル (USD)	ユーロ (EUR)	ユーロ (EUR)	ケニア・シリング (KES)	ユーロ (EUR)	ユーロ (EUR)	ソル (PEN)
立憲君主制・二院制	大統領制・二院制	共和制・一院制	立憲君主制・二院制	共和制・二院制	共和制・二院制	共和制・二院制	立憲共和制・一院制
仏教	キリスト教	キリスト教	キリスト教	キリスト教、イスラム教	キリスト教、イスラム教、ユダヤ教	キリスト教	キリスト教
自動車組立、電子機器、観光、農業	化学薬品、電子機器、自動車、観光、石油・ガス	電子機器、機械、パルプ、金属	化学薬品、機械、金属、食品	農業、食品、繊維、観光	観光、化学薬品、自動車、航空機	化学薬品、IT、金融、食品	鉱業、農業、食品、繊維
ワット・ポー	自由の女神	ヘルシンキ大聖堂	グランプラス	マサイマラ国立保護区	エッフェル塔	モハーの断崖	マチュピチュ
トムヤンクン	ホットドッグ	カレリアパイ	ベルギーワッフル	ウガリ	エスカルゴ	ギネスシチュー	セビーチェ

※関係機関のデータに基づき定期的に情報更新

UNIT 1

Italy — The Start of Pizza Margherita

動詞

イタリアは、地中海の中央に位置しブーツの形をした国土を持つ。その文化、芸術、学問、宗教は世界に影響を与えてきた。モナ・リザを描いたダ・ヴィンチ、天文学者のガリレオ、探検家のコロンブスなど偉人たちの故国である。また、ピザやパスタなどの料理は国際的な食文化の発展に貢献している。

1 Vocabulary

英語に対応する日本語を選びましょう。

1. represent (　　)　　2. prefer (　　)　　3. competition (　　)
4. explore (　　)　　5. texture (　　)

[a] 競争（きょうそう）　[b] 探索する（たんさく）　[c] 食感（しょっかん）　[d] 好む（この）　[e] 象徴する（しょうちょう）

2 Word Mapping

マッピングの空所に合う語句を記入し確認しましょう。

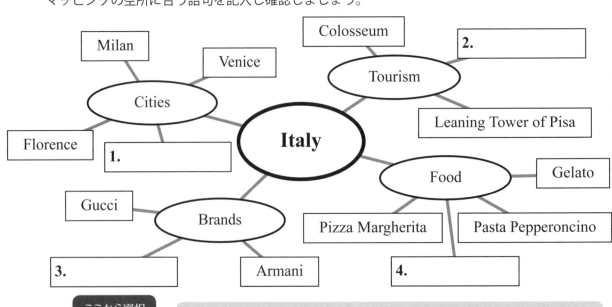

ここから選択しましょう。　Lasagna / Rome / Mouth of Truth / Prada

UNIT 1 **Italy** •The Start of Pizza Margherita

🌐3 Target Grammar

解説を読み文法を学習しましょう。

一般動詞

一般動詞は、具体的な動作や行動について表現することばです。英語の動詞は主語の次に置かれます。

(1) 基本形： S + V + 目的語など

> S (Subject)：主語、
> V (Verb)：動詞です。

I like pasta. パスタが好きです。
We bake cookies. 私たちはクッキーを焼きます。

(2) 三人称・単数・現在

Daniel eats tofu. ダニエルは豆腐を食べます。
It takes time. 時間がかかります。

> ヒントとして日本語が
> 小さく表示されます。

(3) 過去形

She met a famous actor. 彼女は有名な俳優に会いました。
They visited Vatican City. 彼らはバチカン市国を訪れました。

(4) 否定文： S + do/does not + V（原形）

I do not ride roller coasters. ジェットコースターに乗りません。
My poodle does not bark. 私のプードルは吠えません。
We did not watch the game. 私たちはその試合を観ませんでした。

(5) 疑問文： Do/Does + S + V（原形）？

Do you know the shape of Italy? イタリアの形を知っていますか?
Does he attend dance class? 彼はダンスクラスに参加しますか?
Did Maria bring her umbrella? マリアは傘を持ってきましたか?

(6) 疑問文 5W： What + do/does + S + V（原形）？

What do you think? どう思いますか?
When do you listen to music? いつ音楽を聴きますか?
Where do you live? どこに住んでいますか?
Who does she talk to? 彼女は誰と話しますか?
Why does he study hard? なぜ彼は一生懸命勉強しますか?

be 動詞

be 動詞は、 am, is, are, was, were, be, been で、「〜である」という状態や存在を表現します。

11

🌐4 Completing Sentences

選択肢を用いて日本語に沿った文を完成させましょう。

1. I _____ bread for breakfast.
   朝食にパンを食べます。

2. Luca _____ to university four days a week.
   ルカは週に4日間、大学へ行きます。

3. _____ you watch Hollywood movies?
   ハリウッド映画を観ますか?

4. _____ Ms. Evans speak Italian?
   エバンスさんはイタリア語を話しますか?

5. When _____ you arrive here?
   いつ到着しましたか?

ここから選択
しましょう。

do
goes
did
have
does

🌐5 Word Order

語順を並び替え文を完成させましょう。

1. _____ alcohol.

   does / father / not / my / drink

2. Sam _____ night.

   party / last / attended / welcome / the

3. _____ her hometown regularly?

   to / back / she / go / does

4. My _____ the morning.

   up / sister / in / early / wakes

5. _____ own business?

   he / did / why / his / start

❶ トリビアを読み内容を理解しましょう。

The Start of Pizza Margherita

Many people <u>know</u> the name "Margherita" as a type of pizza, but do you <u>know</u> the reason why it is used? The toppings of basil, mozzarella cheese, and tomatoes <u>represent</u> the colors of the Italian flag: green, white, and red.

In 1868, King Umberto the First of Italy <u>married</u> Margherita, and she <u>became</u> the Queen. After they <u>married</u>, she <u>tried</u> to be friendly to everyone. As a result, she was beloved by the public for her friendly personality.

It is said that during a visit to Naples, the King and Queen <u>stopped</u> at a well-known pizza restaurant. They were served a pizza with the colors of the Italian flag. They <u>enjoyed</u> it, so the chef was proud of his pizza and <u>named</u> it after Queen Margherita. Today, pizza Margherita is loved by many people around the world.

◆ as a result: 結果として　◆ it is said that ～ : ～と言われている　◆ be proud of ～ : ～を誇りに思う

❷ 問いに対して最も適切なものを選択しましょう。

1. What do the colors of pizza Margherita refer to?
   [a] The colors of a rainbow　　　　[b] The Queen's memorial colors
   [c] The chef's favorite colors　　　[d] The national colors of Italy

2. Why was the Queen beloved by the public?
   [a] For her fashion sense　　　　[b] For her warm personality
   [c] For her cooking skills　　　　[d] For her musical talent

3. How did the chef react after the King and Queen enjoyed his dish?
   [a] He offered them a discount.
   [b] He decided to open a new restaurant.
   [c] He named the pizza style after the Queen.
   [d] He kept the recipe a secret.

7 Conversation with Listening

❶ 会話の音声を聴きながら英語を記入し内容を理解しましょう。

Elena and **Luigi**: *University students in Rome*

Dinner Invitation

Elena: Hi, Luigi, are you free this evening?

Luigi: Sure, Elena.

Elena: Why don't we (1)_____ dinner tonight?

Luigi: Nice idea. What are you in the mood for?

Elena: I would (2)_____ pasta because it's my favorite food.

Luigi: Wonderful. What kind of pasta do you like?

Elena: I love lasagna. It's full of cheese and meat sauce.

Luigi: I like it too. Have you ever tried making lasagna yourself?

Elena: I tried it once, but it wasn't easy. I just enjoy cooking.

Luigi: Do you (3)_____ often?

Elena: Yes, I like to try new recipes from different countries.

Luigi: I'm sure you must be a good cook. Okay, let's (4)_____ some pasta at my favorite Italian restaurant tonight.

Elena: That's a great choice. Thank you, Luigi.

◆ why don't we V : Vしませんか ◆ be in the mood for ～ : ～の気分である

❷ 文に対して True or False を選択しましょう。

1. Elena suggested having dinner with Luigi.　　True　False
2. Luigi has never tasted lasagna before.　　True　False
3. Elena finds making lasagna very easy.　　True　False
4. Luigi and Elena decide to eat Italian food tonight.　　True　False

UNIT 1   Italy •The Start of Pizza Margherita

8 Presentation

 04

❶ 発表のモデル文を読み内容を理解しましょう。

Marco: *A university student originally from Venice*

My Favorite Food

Nice to meet you, everyone. I'm Marco, originally from Venice. Today, I'd like to talk about my favorite food.

Pasta Pepperoncino is a wonderful dish that I love to eat. It's more than just a meal; it's a part of the culture. I really like its flavor. I usually put olive oil with pepper on it.

Because I love the dish, I eat it once every two weeks. It's not just food to me; it brings joy with every bite. Thank you for listening.

❷ ロールプレイのため英語を記入しペア・グループ内で発表しましょう。

My Favorite Food

波線には自分の情報を書きましょう。

Nice to meet you, everyone. I'm _____, originally from _____. Today, I'd like to talk about my favorite food.

_____ is a wonderful dish that I love to eat. It's more than just a meal; it's a part of the culture. I really like its [1] _____. I usually put [2] _____ with [3] _____ on it.

Because I love the dish, I eat it once

選択肢から選べます。

[4] _____. It's not just food to me; it brings joy with every bite. Thank you for listening.

[1] flavor, taste, texture, smell, style, etc.
[2] ketchup, mayonnaise, olive oil, soy sauce, Worcestershire sauce, etc.
[3] garlic, mustard, pepper, salt, wasabi, etc.
[4] a day, every three days, a week, every two weeks, a month, etc.

15

UNIT 2 Malaysia

The Name of Kuala Lumpur

人称代名詞・冠詞

マレーシアは、マレー系、中華系、インド系の3つの主要民族から構成される人種のるつぼであり、その多民族性が豊かな食文化を生み出している。近年、先進国化を目指しており、常夏のリゾート地がある一方、首都クアラルンプールでは、発展を象徴する巨大ショッピングモールや高層ビルなどが建ち並ぶ。

1 Vocabulary

英語に対応する日本語を選びましょう。

1. commercial (　　)　　2. therefore (　　)　　3. industry (　　)
4. notice (　　)　　5. atmosphere (　　)

[a] 雰囲気　　[b] 商業の　　[c] 気がつく　　[d] 産業　　[e] それゆえ

2 Word Mapping

マッピングの空所に合う語句を記入し確認しましょう。

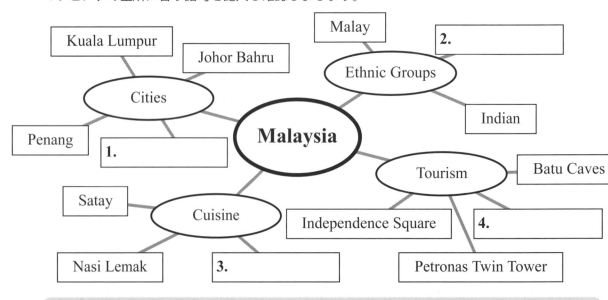

Laksa / Malacca / Chinese / Putra Mosque

16

UNIT 2　**Malaysia** •The Name of Kuala Lumpur

🌐3　Target Grammar

解説を読み文法を学習しましょう。

人称代名詞

人称代名詞は、 I, my, me, mine などであり、前に挙げた人や物の名前を繰り返さずに済む利点があります。

> The students are friendly. They are also smart, so we like them.
> その生徒たちはフレンドリーです。彼らはまた賢いので、私たちは彼らが好きです。

> He bought a guitar. It was expensive, and its sound was excellent.
> 彼はギターを買いました。それは高価で、音が素晴らしかったです。

人称代名詞一覧表

主格	所有格	目的格	所有代名詞
I	my	me	mine
you	your	you	yours
he	his	(　　　)	his
she	(　　　)	her	(　　　)
it	its	(　　　)	——
we	(　　　)	us	(　　　)
they	their	(　　　)	theirs

> 人称代名詞を記入しましょう。

冠詞

冠詞には 不定冠詞の a 、 定冠詞の the があります。

◆ 母音の発音から始まる語には、a の代わりに "an" を使う e.g. an apple

(1) 特定する必要のない**1**つの名詞のには 不定冠詞 "a" を付ける

My uncle owns a boat.　叔父はボートを持っています。
We watched a movie.　私たちは映画を観ました。

(2) 数えられない名詞には "a" を付けない

I like music.　音楽が好きです。
We eat rice.　私たちはお米を食べます。

(3) 概念としての名詞には "a" を付けない

They play basketball.　彼らはバスケットボールをします。
All we need is love.　私たちに必要なのは愛です。

(4) 唯一無二のもの・特定できるものには 定冠詞 "the" を付ける

The Twin Towers are famous.　ツインタワーは有名です。
The sun rises in the east.　太陽は東から昇ります。

🌐4 Completing Sentences

選択肢を用いて日本語に沿った文を完成させましょう。

1. I saw _____ at the shopping mall.
   彼をショッピングモールで見ました。

2. I ordered _____ cup of coffee.
   コーヒーを一杯、注文しました。

3. Malaysian people eat _____ durian.
   マレーシアの人々はドリアンを食べます。

4. Ms. Smith visited _____ home.
   スミスさんは私たちの家を訪れました。

5. Recycling is a way to save _____ earth.
   リサイクルは地球を守る手段です。

our

the

a

him

なし

🌐5 Word Order

語順を並び替え文を完成させましょう。

1. _____ younger brother.

   of / she / care / her / takes

2. _____ Penang.

   an / have / apartment / they / in

3. I _____ the website.

   to / the / access / password / need

4. _____ festival last weekend?

   attend / the / you / cultural / did

5. The _____ feature of Malaysia.

   an / culture / important / is / unique

❶ トリビアを読み内容を理解しましょう。

The Name of Kuala Lumpur

The capital city of Malaysia is Kuala Lumpur or KL for short. It is the cultural, commercial, and transportation center of Malaysia. The reason the city got its name is interesting. In the Malay language, *kuala* means "a meeting point of rivers," and *lumpur* means "mud." Therefore, Kuala Lumpur means "a meeting point of muddy rivers." The city gets its name because it is located where two rivers meet.

In the 1850s, tin miners, including many Chinese, started to come to Kuala Lumpur when it was still a small place. Thanks to the tin mining industry, it grew quickly. This was the beginning of the change from a quiet village to a big and busy city. Today, not only Malays but also Chinese, Indians, and people from other backgrounds live together there, making it a place full of different cultures.

◆ **for short:** 略して ◆ **muddy meeting point:** 泥の交わる場所 ◆ **tin miner:** スズ炭鉱作業員
◆ **thanks to ～:** ～のおかげで

❷ 問いに対して最も適切なものを選択しましょう。

1. What does Kuala Lumpur mean in the Malay language?
   [a] A peaceful heaven land   [b] A cultural exchange center
   [c] A central city avenue   [d] A meeting point of muddy rivers

2. What was the reason for the growth of KL in the mid-19th century?
   [a] The spice trade   [b] The tin mining industry
   [c] Rubber plantations   [d] A tourism boom

3. How did KL change over the years?
   [a] From a busy city to a quiet village
   [b] From a quiet village to a busy city
   [c] From a trading port to a limited cultural hub
   [d] From an urban center to a peaceful community

7 Conversation with Listening

❶ 会話の音声を聴きながら英語を記入し内容を理解しましょう。

Imran and **Lily**: *University students in Putrajaya*

Hometown Connection

Imran: Hi, Lily, how are you doing?
Lily: Hi, I'm doing well, thanks.
Imran: Can I ask where (1)_____ are from?
Lily: I'm from Penang.
Imran: Really? Actually, Penang is a place I'd like to visit.
Lily: Why do you want to go there?
Imran: I major in tourism, and one of my projects relates to the resort industry.
Lily: Yes, Penang is one of (2)_____ most popular resorts in Malaysia, but what will you do there?
Imran: Well, I was in Malacca last month, and I interviewed some local people working at hotels and restaurants. Now, I want to do the same thing in Penang.
Lily: I see. So, you gathered real opinions from local people. Did you notice any trends?
Imran: Definitely. It was very helpful for my project.
Lily: Okay, so now I understand what you aim to do in Penang. When you go, please let (3)_____ know. I have some friends who work there, so I can give you their contact information.
Imran: Really?
Lily: I'm sure that (4)_____ would love to help you.
Imran: That's great. I can't thank you enough.

◆ **major in ～**: ～を専攻する　◆ **definitely:** もちろん

❷ 文に対して True [T] or False [F] を選択しましょう。

1. Imran majors in economics at his university.　T F
2. Imran noticed some trends when he interviewed people in Malacca.　T F
3. Lily offered to introduce Imran to her friends in Penang.　T F
4. Imran and Lily plan to travel to Penang together.　T F

UNIT 2　Malaysia ●The Name of Kuala Lumpur

 07

❶ 発表のモデル文を読み内容を理解しましょう。

Aina: A university student from Kuala Lumpur

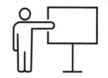

My Hometown

Hello, everyone. I'm Aina from Kuala Lumpur. Today, I'd like to introduce my hometown.

Kuala Lumpur is located in the west of Selangor. What I love the most about my hometown is its comfortable atmosphere. It's a welcoming oasis for me. It has a lot of shops and modern structures. When you are hungry, I recommend Chinese food; there are some excellent restaurants in the area.

My hometown is a peaceful and safe place, where my spirit feels at home. Thank you for listening.

◆ **welcoming oasis:** 心地よいオアシス

❷ ロールプレイのため英語を記入しペア・グループ内で発表しましょう。

My Hometown

Hello, everyone. I'm ＿＿＿＿＿＿ from ＿＿＿＿＿＿. Today, I'd like to introduce my hometown.

＿＿＿＿＿＿ is located [1]＿＿＿＿＿＿. What I love the most about my hometown is its comfortable atmosphere. It's a welcoming oasis for me. It has a lot of [2]＿＿＿＿＿＿. When you are hungry, I recommend [3]＿＿＿＿＿＿ food; there are some excellent restaurants in the area.

My hometown is a peaceful and safe place, where my spirit feels at home. Thank you for listening.

---

[1] in the north of Miyagi, in a suburb of Chiba, near Nagoya, etc.

[2] beaches and mountains, trees and rivers, stores and tall buildings, etc.

[3] Japanese, Chinese, Korean, Italian, French, Indian, etc.

The UK The Beatles Audition

UNIT 3

助動詞

イギリスは、現代の社会基盤を作った国であり、さまざまな社会システムが各国に広がっている。また、その文化・伝統の多くは現代にも受け継がれ、世界中の人々を魅了する。イギリス（英国）の正式名称は、The United Kingdom of Great Britain and Northern Ireland（グレートブリテン及び北アイルランド連合王国）である。

1 Vocabulary

英語に対応する日本語を選びましょう。

1. submit (   )   2. reject (   )   3. unknown (   )
4. contract (   ) 5. confident (   )

[a] 契約   [b] 自信がある   [c] 却下する   [d] 知られていない   [e] 提出する

2 Word Mapping

マッピングの空所に合う語句を記入し確認しましょう。

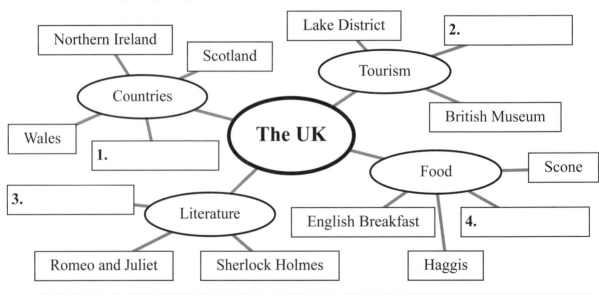

London Eye / Fish and Chips / Harry Potter / England

UNIT 3　The UK ●The Beatles Audition

3　Target Grammar

解説を読み文法を学習しましょう。

助動詞

助動詞を用いることで、動詞のニュアンスを変化させ、話者の意思を細かく伝えることができます。

(1) 基本文： S + 助動詞 + V（原形）

I <u>will</u> meet my friend.　友達に会うつもりです。
She <u>can</u> play golf.　彼女はゴルフができます。
My brother <u>should</u> clean his room.　弟は部屋を掃除すべきです。

(2) 否定文： S + 助動詞 not + V（原形）

He <u>will not</u> go there.　彼はそこへ行かないでしょう。
We <u>can not</u> change the plan.　私たちはその計画を変更できません。
They <u>should not</u> be late.　彼らは遅れるべきではありません。

(3) 疑問文： 助動詞 + S + V（原形）？

<u>Will</u> you have lunch?　ランチをとりますか？
<u>Can</u> Sally play the piano?　サリーはピアノを弾けますか？
<u>Should</u> I take off my hat?　帽子を脱ぐべきですか？

(4) 意思の強弱の比較

I _____ attend the party.

must	〜しなければならない
should	〜するべきである
will	〜つもりである
can	〜できる
may	〜かもしれない
won't	〜しないだろう
can't	〜するはずがない

◆ won't: will not
◆ can't: can not, cannot

(5) 関連表現

`want to` と `would like to` を比べると、"want to" はカジュアルで直接的な表現で、"would like to" はフォーマルで丁寧な表現となります。
I'<u>d like to</u> introduce my hometown.　地元を紹介したいと思います。

`must` と `have to` を比べると、"must" は話者自身の意思や要求を伝えるときに好まれ、"have to" は外部からの規則や義務を伝えるのに好まれます。
I <u>have to</u> submit the end-of-term report.　期末レポートを提出しなければなりません。

🌐4 Completing Sentences

選択肢を用いて日本語に沿った文を完成させましょう。

1. I _____ do my homework.
   宿題をしなければなりません。

2. I _____ dance well.
   上手く踊れません。

3. She _____ buy a new bag.
   彼女は新しいバッグを買うかもしれません。

4. We _____ forget the exam day.
   私たちは試験日を忘れてはいけません。

5. _____ you sing the song Yesterday?
   Yesterday という曲を歌えますか?

can
may
mustn't
have to
can't

🌐5 Word Order

語順を並び替え文を完成させましょう。

1. Allen _____ the audition.

   must / to / practice / pass / hard

2. We _____ by Friday.

   the / to / report / have / submit

3. I guess _____.

   the / be / rumor / true / can't

4. _____ name?

   your / I / ask / may / family

5. _____ 9 AM.

   store / open / the / won't / until

6 Reading Trivia

❶ トリビアを読み内容を理解しましょう。

The Beatles Audition

What was the biggest mistake in the music industry? It <u>might be</u> the decision by Decca Records to reject the Beatles after their audition. At that time, the members were young, unknown musicians. Their manager, Brian Epstein, tried to get a recording contract for them.

Decca invited them to perform an audition on January 1st, 1962, and the Beatles recorded 15 songs at a studio in London. A month later, Decca contacted Epstein with an unbelievable answer: the company <u>wouldn't sign</u> the band. It was reported that the person in charge told Epstein that "guitar groups are on the way out" and "the Beatles have no future in show business."

However, a few months later, George Martin, a producer at the record company EMI, listened to the audition tape. After he asked the company to offer the Beatles a contract, the band signed with EMI on June 18th, 1962, and the rest is history.

◆ **be on the way out:** 時代遅れである ◆ **the rest is history:** 後は知ってのとおり

❷ 問いに対して最も適切なものを選択しましょう。

1. What was Brian Epstein's aim at the beginning of 1962?
   [a] To make the Beatles successful [b] To become a member of the Beatles
   [c] To listen to the Beatles' songs. [d] To sell many kinds of products

2. What was Decca's comment about the Beatles?
   [a] They should use more guitars.
   [b] They do not have a future.
   [c] They will be successful.
   [d] One member should be replaced.

3. What happened on June 18th, 1962?
   [a] The Beatles played 15 songs at a studio.
   [b] The Beatles tried to persuade a producer to record them.
   [c] The Beatles signed a contract with a recording company.
   [d] The Beatles listened to an audition tape in the studio.

7 Conversation with Listening

❶ 会話の音声を聴きながら英語を記入し内容を理解しましょう。

Jack and *Emma*: University students in Birmingham

Joining a Band

Jack: Hello, Emma. (1)_____ I ask you something?
Emma: Yes, of course, Jack.
Jack: I'm a member of a music club, and we are planning to perform some songs at the welcome party for the new dormitory members.
Emma: That sounds great.
Jack: The venue is Apple Hall on campus, and the event is in two months.
Emma: Oh, fantastic! What musical instrument do you play?
Jack: I play the guitar, and we already have a bassist and a drummer.
Emma: That's cool.
Jack: But we also need a vocalist. (2)_____ you sing a few songs with us?
Emma: Me?
Jack: Yes, I know you are a good singer. Why don't we perform some songs together?
Emma: Well, Jack, I'm not really confident about singing in front of an audience.
Jack: Don't worry. You (3)_____ use the music room to practice as much as you like.
Emma: Well, (4)_____ it be okay to get back to you later?
Jack: No problem. It's up to you. We have plenty of time.

◆ musical instrument: 楽器　◆ as much as you like: 好きなだけ
◆ get back to you later: 改めて返事する

❷ 文に対して True [T] or False [F] を選択しましょう。

1. The welcome party will be held outside of the university. [T] [F]

2. Including Jack, there are three band members so far. [T] [F]

3. Emma finds it easy to sing songs in front of a large number of people. [T] [F]

4. Emma finally decided to perform with Jack's band. [T] [F]

UNIT 3　The UK ●The Beatles Audition

 **Presentation**

❶ 発表のモデル文を読み内容を理解しましょう。

Steven: *A university student in Liverpool*

Musical Instrument

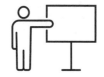

Hello. I'm Steven. I'd like to learn how to play a musical instrument. My first choice is the guitar. I like the sound of it, and I have heard it's not difficult to play. I may buy a guitar this summer, so I'm working part-time to earn money.

My second choice is the bass. It's important to keep a steady rhythm. We can say, "no bass, no music."

My favorite music is British rock, and my favorite band is Queen. One of my friends asked me to join his band, and I'd like to play some songs with him. In the future, though, I hope I can play solo on the stage. Thank you for listening.

---

❷ ロールプレイのため英語を記入しペア・グループ内で発表しましょう。

Musical Instrument

Hello. I'm _____. I'd like to learn how to play a musical instrument. My first choice is the [1]_____. I like the sound of it, and I have heard it's not difficult to play. I may buy a [1]_____ this summer, so I'm working part-time to earn money.

My second choice is the [2]_____. It's important to keep a steady rhythm. We can say, "no [2]_____, no music."

My favorite music is [3]_____, and my favorite band/singer is _____. One of my friends asked me to join his/her band, and I'd like to play some songs with him/her. In the future, though, I hope I can play solo on the stage. Thank you for listening.

---

[1] guitar, keyboard, piano, trumpet, violin, etc.

[2] drums, percussion, bass, contrabass, tambourine, etc.

[3] British rock, American pop, J-pop, K-pop, hard rock, hip-hop, etc.

Egypt

UNIT 4

Exploring the Great Sphinx

受動態

エジプトは、中東とアフリカ大陸を結ぶ位置にある。アラブ諸国で最も人口が多く、1億人を超えている。国民の約9割がイスラム教を信仰し、国教に定められている。古代文明の発祥の地の一つで、首都カイロにあるギザのピラミッドなど、多くの遺跡が点在し世界的に有名な観光名所となっている。

1 Vocabulary

英語に対応する日本語を選びましょう。

1. guardian (　　)　　2. ancient (　　)　　3. fascinating (　　)
4. envy (　　)　　5. appearance (　　)

[a] 外見　　[b] うらやむ　　[c] 守護神　　[d] 魅力的な　　[e] 古代の

2 Word Mapping

マッピングの空所に合う語句を記入し確認しましょう。

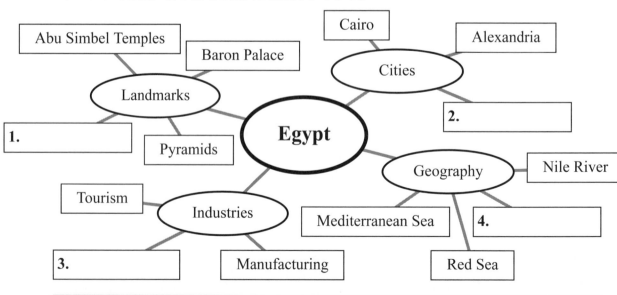

Giza / Sphinx / Sahara Desert / Oil and Gas

UNIT 4　**Egypt** ●Exploring the Great Sphinx

🌐3　Target Grammar

解説を読み文法を学習しましょう。

受動態

受動態の文は、「（主語は）〜される」という表現となり、能動態の文の目的語を主語に置き換えることができます。基本形は、 主語 + be 動詞 + 過去分詞 です。「誰・何によって」と明言する場合は、by 〜を加えます。

能動態と受動態の比較

	（主語）	（動詞）	（目的語）
能動態	Ancient Egyptians	built	the Sphinx.

受動態	The Sphinx	was built	by Ancient Egyptians.
	（主語）	（be 動詞 + 過去分詞）	（by 誰・何）

スフィンクスは古代エジプト人によって建てられました。

(1) 過去の事実： S + was/were + 過去分詞 + by 誰・何

The party was held by the student union.
　　パーティーは学生組合によって開催されました。

Our mailbox was broken by the typhoon.　郵便受けは台風によって壊されました。

The new smartphones were released by the company.
　　新しいスマートフォンはその企業からリリースされました。

副詞句をともなった文

His bicycle was stolen last week.　彼の自転車は先週盗まれました。

Microsoft was started by Bill Gates in 1975.
　　マイクロソフトは 1975 年にビル・ゲイツによって創業されました。

The blueberries in my garden were eaten by birds.
　　庭のブルーベリーは鳥に食べられました。

(2) 継続的行動： S + is/are + 過去分詞 + by 誰・何

Information is provided by the website.　情報はウェブサイトから提供されます。

Advice is given by my supervisor.　アドバイスは上司から与えられます。

Dishes are washed by my father.　食器は父が洗います。

副詞句をともなった文

Breakfast is cooked by my sister every day.　朝食は毎日妹が作ります。

My guitar is always tuned by Tim.　私のギターはいつもティムがチューニングします。

Emails are usually sent by office clerks.　メールは通常、事務員によって送信されます。

4 Completing Sentences

語句を用いて日本語に沿った受動態の文を完成させましょう。

1. The music studio _____ _____ by the staff. (close)
   音楽スタジオはスタッフが閉めます。

2. The artwork _____ _____ by Henry. (create)
   そのアート作品はヘンリーによって作られました。

3. My desserts _____ sometimes _____ by my sister. (eat)
   時々、妹にデザートを食べられます。

4. The song _____ _____ by Ms. Taylor five years ago. (compose)
   その歌は5年前、テイラーさんにより作られました。

5. Training sessions _____ always _____ by the support desk.
   トレーニングセッションはいつもサポートデスクにより実施されます。　　　(conduct)

5 Word Order

語順を並び替え文を完成させましょう。

1. The _____ father every day.

   is / my / cleaned / bathroom / by

2. _____ Ms. Evans.

   the / given / was / by / presentation

3. My _____ bicycle yesterday.

   was / brother / a / by / hit

4. _____ Daisy in the cafe.

   always / by / meals / cooked / are

5. The _____ Mr. Ali this year.

   by / taught / Arabic / is / course

❶ トリビアを読み内容を理解しましょう。

Exploring the Great Sphinx

The Great Sphinx of Giza in Egypt, the largest statue in the world, is a legendary guardian, with a human head and a lion's body. It is a popular sightseeing spot, attracting many tourists. It is about 72 meters long and 20 meters high and was built about 4,500 years ago. Originally, the site was a quarry, and the Sphinx was carved out from the rock beneath. The mysterious structure always gets the attention of many researchers.

The Sphinx was often buried by sand because it was at the lowest point in the area. In 1818, while removing sand, researchers found a stone monument called the "Dream Stele" containing ancient script between the Sphinx's front paws. This monument was built by Thutmose the Fourth about 3,400 years ago. The following words were written on the monument: "Thutmose the Fourth was asleep under the Sphinx's shadow. In his dream, a god told him to remove the sand and clean the Sphinx. He followed the instructions and became king."

The Sphinx is still known as a fascinating subject for research because of its many mysteries.

◆ quarry: 石切り場　◆ be carved out: 削りだされる　◆ Dream Stele: 夢の石碑

❷ 問いに対して最も適切なものを選択しましょう。

1. What discovery was made by researchers in 1818?
   [a] A treasure box　　　　[b] The Rosetta Stone
   [c] A dinosaur bone　　　[d] The Dream Stele

2. According to the monument, what did Thutmose the Fourth dream about?
   [a] Building a pyramid　　[b] Defeating enemies in battle
   [c] Cleaning the Sphinx　　[d] Finding buried treasure

3. What happened to the Great Sphinx over the years?
   [a] It was destroyed by an earthquake.　　[b] It was covered by sand.
   [c] It was moved to another location.　　　[d] It was damaged by water.

7 Conversation with Listening

❶ 会話の音声を聴きながら英語を記入し内容を理解しましょう。

Mohamed and *Farida*: University students in Alexandria

My Stay Near the Pyramids of Giza

Mohamed: Hi, Farida! I traveled to Giza to see the Pyramids last weekend.
Farida: Really? That's a fascinating spot. Where did you stay?
Mohamed: I stayed at a hotel close to the Great Sphinx. It was only a 10-minute walk from there.
Farida: Wow, that's close!
Mohamed: The pyramids could be (1)_____ from my hotel window.
Farida: Oh, you were lucky. How was the food there?
Mohamed: Traditional Egyptian meals were (2)_____ at the hotel. They were all delicious.
Farida: That sounds great. By the way, did you go inside the pyramids?
Mohamed: Yes, I went into the Pyramid of Khufu.
Farida: I have heard that the pyramid was (3)_____ 4,500 years ago.
Mohamed: Yes, I explored inside the pyramid for 30 minutes.
Farida: How was it?
Mohamed: Actually, it was quite hot inside, but I was really (4)_____.
Farida: I envy you. It sounds like you had a memorable trip.
Mohamed: Absolutely! It was the best trip of my life.
Farida: I should definitely visit Giza sometime.
Mohamed: Yes, you should. I will let you know the best things to do in Giza when you visit.
Farida: Thank you, Mohamed. You are very kind.

◆ **be in the mood for** ～ : ～の気分である

❷ 文に対して True [T] or False [F] を選択しましょう。

1. Farida has recently visited the Pyramids of Giza. [T] [F]
2. Mohamed enjoyed traditional Egyptian food at a local restaurant. [T] [F]
3. Farida knows the Pyramid of Khufu was built 4,500 years ago. [T] [F]
4. It was cold inside the Pyramid of Khufu when Mohamed explored it. [T] [F]

UNIT 4 Egypt • Exploring the Great Sphinx

 **Presentation**   13

❶ 発表のモデル文を読み内容を理解しましょう。

Hana: A university student in Cairo

My Favorite Landmark

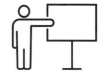

Hello, I'm Hana. Today, it's my pleasure to talk about my favorite landmark, Baron Palace. It's located in Cairo and was built more than 100 years ago. The design of this structure always holds my attention. I'm always inspired by its appearance whenever I see it.

When I visit, the atmosphere of the place makes me feel amazed. It reminds me that I can do great things.

I hope you get to see it one day, and I'm sure that you will be impressed by the landmark. I encourage you to visit it if you have the chance. Thank you for listening.

---

❷ ロールプレイのため英語を記入しペア・グループ内で発表しましょう。

My Favorite Landmark

Hello, I'm _____. Today, it's my pleasure to talk about my favorite landmark, _____. It's located in _____ and was built [1]_____ ago. The design of this structure always holds my attention. I'm always inspired by its [2]_____ whenever I see it.

When I visit, the atmosphere of the place makes me feel [3]_____. It reminds me that I can do great things.

I hope you get to see it one day, and I'm sure that you will be [4]_____ by the landmark. I encourage you to visit it if you have the chance. Thank you for listening.

---

[1] half a year, five years, around 10 years, more than 30 years, etc.
[2] beauty, elegance, harmony, presence, scale, shape, strength, etc.
[3] cheerful, hopeful, nostalgic, peaceful, relaxed, comfortable, etc.
[4] excited, fascinated, impressed, moved, surprised, touched, etc.

33

UNIT 5

Germany — Founders of Adidas and Puma

現在完了

ドイツは、第二次世界大戦後に東西の対立により2つに分断されたが、1989年11月9日、東ドイツ人民の旅行規制の緩和が発表されたことを機に、市民が歓喜しベルリンの壁崩壊がおこり、翌年、ドイツ連邦共和国として統一された。現在、EUの中で最も人口の多い経済大国である。ドイツ語の国名はDeutschlandである。

1 Vocabulary

英語に対応する日本語を選びましょう。

1. shed (　　) 2. founder (　　) 3. affect (　　)
4. struggle (　　) 5. conflict (　　)

[a] 創設者　[b] 影響する　[c] 対立　[d] 小屋　[e] 奮闘

2 Word Mapping

マッピングの空所に合う語句を記入し確認しましょう。

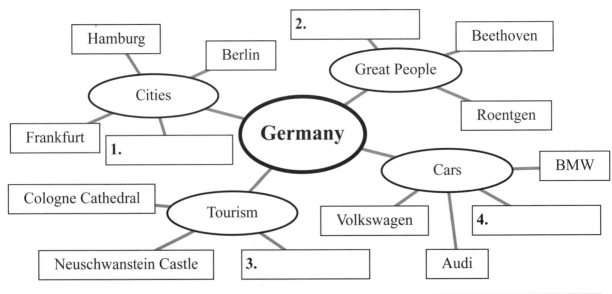

Mercedes / Einstein / Munich / Oktoberfest

UNIT 5　Germany •Founders of Adidas and Puma

 Target Grammar

解説を読み文法を学習しましょう。

現在完了

現在完了は、過去の出来事が現在に関連している場合に使われる表現です。話者（主語）の「経験」「継続」「完了」「結果」について述べ、現在までのつながりを示します。

過去形　I cooked German potatoes last month.
先月、ジャーマンポテトを作りました。

現在完了　I have learned German for a month.
1ヵ月間、ドイツ語を学んでいます。

(1) 基本形： S + have/has + 過去分詞

I have lost my student ID card.　学生証を失くしてしまいました。
She has practiced the guitar for two years.　彼女は2年間ギターを練習しています。
They have lived in the house for 10 years.　彼らは10年間その家に住んでいます。

(2) 否定文： S + have/has not + 過去分詞

I have not watched the movie.　その映画を観ていません。
Eric has not eaten natto.　エリックは納豆を食べたことがありません。
We have not met the new teacher.　私たちは新しい先生にまだ会っていません。

(3) 疑問文： Have/Has + S + 過去分詞？

Have you cleaned your room?　部屋を掃除しましたか？
Have you submitted the report?　レポートを提出しましたか？
Has he found his passport?　彼はパスポートを見つけましたか？

不規則動詞一覧表（現在－過去－過去分詞）　　　　　　　　　　　過去分詞を記入しましょう。

begin	began	begun
come	came	(　　)
drive	drove	driven
forget	forgot	(　　)
give	gave	given

put	put	(　　)
know	knew	known
ride	rode	(　　)
speak	spoke	spoken
throw	threw	(　　)

35

🌐4 Completing Sentences

語句を用いて日本語に沿った現在完了の文を完成させましょう。

1. I _____ _____ him for five years. (know)
   5年間、彼を知っています。

2. She _____ _____ her university life. (enjoy)
   彼女は大学生活を楽しんでいます。

3. _____ you _____ the new novel? (read)
   その新しい小説を読みましたか？

4. I _____ not _____ the meeting after school. (forget)
   放課後、ミーティングがあるのを忘れていません。

5. The sightseeing spot _____ _____ popular since its opening. (be)
   その観光スポットは旅行客に人気です。

🌐5 Word Order

語順を並び替え文を完成させましょう。

1. My _____ 30 years.

   for / taught / has / piano / grandmother

2. I _____ now.

   eaten / until / not / anything / have

3. _____ European countries?

   ever / you / have / any / visited

4. We _____ wall.

   shed / finished / the / have / painting

5. _____ around the world for many years.

   cars / been / German / popular / have

UNIT 5　**Germany** ●Founders of Adidas and Puma

6 Reading Trivia　CD 14

❶ トリビアを読み内容を理解しましょう。

Founders of Adidas and Puma

As everyone knows, the German companies Adidas and Puma <u>have been</u> top sports brands worldwide for many years. However, it may be surprising to know that they were originally the same company. Its founders, the brothers Adolf and Rudolf Dassler, started by sewing sneakers in a room in their home in a small town.

They formed a company called "Geda" in 1919. The turning point came at the Berlin Olympics in 1936, when around a dozen medal winners wore their shoes. However, during World War II, strong competition developed between the brothers. The situation affected thier employees and split the townspeople into two groups. The struggle led them to set up their own companies: Puma in 1948, and Adidas in 1949.

Today, the companies are still in the same place, but relations <u>have become</u> much friendlier in recent years. To avoid conflict, the mayor of the town <u>has decided</u> to wear products made by both companies.

◆ **split A into two groups:** Aを2つのグループに分ける　◆ **set up:** 設立する

❷ 問いに対して最も適切なものを選択しましょう。

1. What happened to the original company in 1936?
   [a] They held a sports event.　　[b] They went bankrupt.
   [c] They started a business.　　[d] They supplied shoes to medal winners.

2. Why did the brothers split Geda into two companies?
   [a] They became friendlier.　　[b] They were happy working together.
   [c] They respected each other.　[d] They had a struggle.

3. What would the mayor probably say about the two brands in a public speech?
   [a] I prefer one over the other.　　　　[b] I can wear only one of them.
   [c] I should not choose between them.　[d] I dislike one of them.

7 Conversation with Listening

 15

❶ 会話の音声を聴きながら英語を記入し内容を理解しましょう。

Lena and Max: University students in Berlin

Sports and Exercise

Lena: Hi, Max, have you ever done any sports?

Max: Yes, I have (1)_____ football for 12 years since I was in elementary school.

Lena: Oh, so you still play football now.

Max: Yes, that's right. Now, I'm a member of the football club at my university.

Lena: I see. You must be good at it.

Max: Well, I do my best. How about you? Have you ever (2)_____ any sports?

Lena: I played tennis for a short time, but now I just walk long distances for my health.

Max: Good idea. I think walking is the perfect exercise.

Lena: I usually get off the train one stop before my destination.

Max: Really? Have you (3)_____ yourself a daily target distance?

Lena: I try to walk 15,000 steps a day. I have (4)_____ this for about half a year.

Max: That's impressive!

◆ be in the mood for 〜 : 〜の気分である

❷ 文に対して True or False を選択しましょう。

1. Max started playing football when he was in kindergarten. True False
2. Max is a member of a football team. True False
3. Lena has never played any ball games before. True False
4. Lena has set a goal for her daily exercise. True False

38

 **Presentation** 16

❶ 発表のモデル文を読み内容を理解しましょう。

Sophie: *A university student in Hamburg*

My Favorite Sports

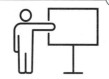

Hello. I'm Sophie. Today, I'm going to talk about my favorite sports.

I have played basketball for eight years. I started when I was in elementary school. I think I'm good at dribbling and passing. Now, I'm a member of the basketball club at my university. Although our team is not so strong, we regularly participate in some local tournaments and try to win our games.

In addition, I have enjoyed watching figure skating since I was very young. When my favorite athletes perform well, I'm happy to cheer for them. Thank you for listening.

❷ ロールプレイのため英語を記入しペア・グループ内で発表しましょう。

My Favorite Sports

Hello. I'm _____. Today, I'm going to talk about my favorite sports.

I have [1]_____ for _____ years. I started it when I was in [2]_____ school. I think I'm good at [3]_____. Now, I'm a member of the [1]_____ club at my university. Although our team is not so strong, we regularly participate in some local tournaments and try to win our games.

In addition, I have enjoyed watching [4]_____ since I was very young. When my favorite athletes perform well, I'm happy to cheer for them. Thank you for listening.

[1] (played) baseball, soccer, tennis, (practiced) karate, judo, etc.
[2] elementary, junior high, high, etc.
[3] hitting and running, dribbling and shooting, serving and smashing, receiving and attacking, defending and kicking, etc.
[4] figure skating, NBA, MLB, WBC, Premier League, the Soccer World Cup, marathons, the Hakone Ekiden, etc.

UNIT 6

New Zealand / The Haka Dance Legacy

進行形

ニュージーランドは、南北2つの主要な島と、多くの小さな島々から構成される。首都はウェリントンだがオークランドが最大都市である。1300年以前にマオリ人の祖先が移住したとい言われる。1769年にキャプテン・クックが島を調査し、その後、英国植民地となり移民が進み、1947年に独立国となる。英語とマオリ語の他に手話が公用語になっている。

1 Vocabulary

英語に対応する日本語を選びましょう。

1. legacy (　　)　　2. commonly (　　)　　3. initially (　　)
4. tribe (　　)　　5. express (　　)

[a] 初めに　　[b] 遺産　　[c] 表現する　　[d] 一般に　　[e] 部族

2 Word Mapping

マッピングの空所に合う語句を記入し確認しましょう。

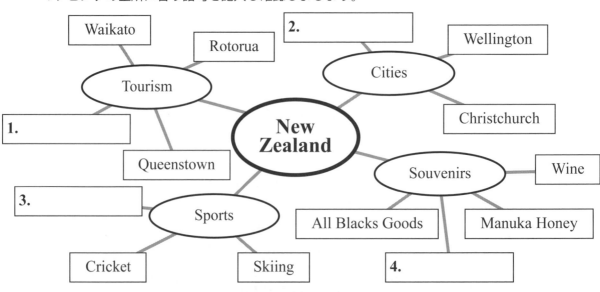

Auckland / Wool Products / Rugby / Lake Tekapo

解説を読み文法を学習しましょう。

> 進行形

進行形は、「進行中の動作」や「一時的に継続している状態」を表現します。「〜している最中」というイメージとなります。基本形は、 主語 + be 動詞 + V-ing で、過去、現在、未来の時制で使えます。

(1) 過去進行形： S + was/were + V-ing

I was watching a movie.　映画を観ていました。
We were playing rugby.　私たちはラグビーをしていました。
（否定）I was not reading a book.　本を読んでいませんでした。
（疑問）Were they singing?　彼らは歌っていましたか？

(2) 現在進行形： S + is/are + V-ing

I am studying English.　英語を勉強しています。
They are enjoying skiing.　彼らはスキーを楽しんでいます。
（否定）We are not working today.　私たちは今日は働いていません。
（疑問）Are you crying?　泣いていますか？

(3) 未来進行形： S + will be + V-ing

It will be raining tomorrow.　明日、雨が降っているでしょう。
We will be having dinner at 7 PM.　私たちは7時に夕食をとっているでしょう。
（否定）He will not be spending any money.　彼はお金を使わないでしょう。
（疑問）Will they be traveling to Rotorua this weekend?
　　　週末、彼らはロトルアに旅行に行く予定ですか？

(4) 近い未来の表現（未来を表す副詞句をともなう）

We are leaving for Queenstown tomorrow.
　　明日、私たちはクイーンズタウンへ向かいます。
Kate is visiting her grandparents next week.　来週、ケイトは祖父母を訪ねます。

(5) 動作動詞と状態動詞

進行形の表現に 動作動詞：play, run, write, etc. は使えますが、 状態動詞：know, like, see, smell, understand, want, etc. は使えません。
We are having lunch.　私たちは今、ランチをとっています。
◆ have は「食べる」では進行形になるが「持つ」では使えない　e.g. We are having a cat.
I am living in Auckland.　私はオークランドに住んでいます。
◆ 自宅は他所にあるが、大学や仕事のため一時的にその場所に住んでいる場合は使える

🌐4 Completing Sentences

語句を用いて日本語に沿った進行形の文を完成させましょう。

1. The baby _____ _____ peacefully. (sleep)

   赤ちゃんは すやすやと眠っています。

2. I _____ not _____ in the office yesterday. (work)

   昨日、オフィスで働いていませんでした。

3. We will _____ _____ for you for a long time. (wait)

   私たちはあなたをいつまでも待っているでしょう。

4. _____ you _____ dance this morning? (practice)

   今朝、ダンスを練習していましたか?

5. Will you _____ _____ the washing machine this evening? (use)

   今晩、洗濯機を使う予定ですか?

🌐5 Word Order

語順を並び替え文を完成させましょう。

1. _____ spring.

   are / hot / we / the / enjoying

2. My _____ right now.

   games / playing / not / is / brother

3. Lucy and _____ the garden.

   wine / Matt / drinking / in / were

4. _____ about Oceania?

   a / you / writing / are / report

5. _____ New Zealand this summer.

   traveling / be / they / in / will

6 Reading Trivia

❶ トリビアを読み内容を理解しましょう。

The Haka Dance Legacy

The Haka is a traditional dance of the Maori, the indigenous people of New Zealand. It is commonly understood to represent the blessing of life. The Maori culture did not use written language initially, and communication was expressed through dances. They are keeping their traditions alive through the Haka.

When thinking of the Haka, rugby is probably the first thing that comes to mind. The New Zealand national team, the All Blacks, has attracted worldwide attention by performing the "Ka Mate," their traditional war cry, before games.

Originally, the Ka Mate was a dance performed by the Maori to display their power to opposing tribes. However, performing the Ka Mate before a match expresses a sense of respect for their opponents, particularly in international matches. Since this is a song for warriors, the meaning of the lyrics is special. For example, the first line is as follows: "Ka mate, ka mate (I die, I die), Ka ora, ka ora (I live, I live)."

In the final part, they are singing, "Step forward into the sun." The Maori are expressing their strength and harmony with nature.

◆ **indigenous people:** 先住民　◆ **blessing of life:** 人生の祝福　◆ **come to mind:** 思い浮かぶ
◆ **war cry:** おたけび　◆ **opposing tribe:** 敵対する部族

❷ 問いに対して最も適切なものを選択しましょう。

1. How did the Maori communicate before the use of written language?
   [a] Speech and painting   [b] Writing and speech
   [c] Speech and dance   [d] Tattoos and speech

2. What was the original purpose of the Ka Mate?
   [a] To express love and affection   [b] To entertain audiences
   [c] To celebrate victory in battles [d] To display power to opposing tribes

3. What aspect of nature do the Maori highlight in their traditional dance?
   [a] The sun   [b] Rivers
   [c] The moon   [d] Forests

7 Conversation with Listening

❶ 会話の音声を聴きながら英語を記入し内容を理解しましょう。

Leo and *Sophie*: University students in Auckland

Dance Club

Leo: Hello, Sophie. Why are you (1)_____?
Sophie: Hi, Leo. I'm (2)_____ an audience for the performance of our dance club.
Leo: Okay, I got it.
Sophie: It's starting soon at Kiwi Hall. Would you like to come and watch it?
Leo: I see. Yes, that sounds fun. What kind of dance will it be?
Sophie: Do you know hip-hop? It started in the Bronx, New York, in the 1970s. It's connected to street culture.
Leo: That's interesting. I have never watched a hip-hop performance before.
Sophie: You should come! It's important for the members to move together when they dance in a group.
Leo: It sounds really enjoyable.
Sophie: The performance is about to start. The hip-hop group is on the stage.
Leo: The street clothes look cool.
Sophie: The leader is (3)_____ in the center.
Leo: They are really good. Aren't you going to dance?
Sophie: No, I have just started learning, but I'm (4)_____ to join in next time.
Leo: Please let me know when you dance!

---

❷ 文に対して True or False を選択しましょう

1. Sophie invites Leo to watch the performance.   True / False
2. Hip-hop originally started in New York.   True / False
3. The hip-hop dancers wear suits and ties.   True / False
4. Sophie is one of the performers this time.   True / False

UNIT 6　**New Zealand** •The Haka Dance Legacy

8 Presentation

❶ 発表のモデル文を読み内容を理解しましょう。

Emma: *A university student in Wellington*

Dance Experience

Hello. I'm Emma. I'm here today to talk about dance. I first danced when I was eight years old. Since then, I have loved dancing and do it regularly. I believe dancing helps people escape the stress of everyday life.

Although I don't stick to a particular genre, I usually dance to popular songs. Therefore, my style may be classified as "pop dance." It's enjoyable because it allows me to express my emotions freely.

I sometimes dance with a few friends in the space in front of A Building. We were dancing yesterday as well. I'm not aiming to be a professional dancer, but dancing is my fun hobby. Now, shall we dance? Thank you for listening.

❷ ロールプレイのため英語を記入しペア・グループ内で発表しましょう。

Dance Experience

Hello. I'm _____. I'm here today to talk about dance. I first danced when I was _____ years old. Since then, I have loved dancing and do it regularly. I believe dancing helps people escape the stress of everyday life.

Although I don't stick to a particular genre, I usually dance to [1]_____. Therefore, my style may be classified as "[2]_____." It's enjoyable because it allows me to express my emotions freely.

I sometimes dance with a few friends in the space in front of A Building. We were dancing yesterday as well. I'm not aiming to be a professional dancer, but dancing is my [3]_____. Now, shall we dance? Thank you for listening.

[1] popular songs, rap, blues, EDM, ballads, classical music, etc.
[2] pop dance, hip-hop dance, jazz dance, breakdance, waltz, ballet, etc.
[3] physical fitness, stress buster, path of freedom, fun hobby, etc.

45

Thailand — The Land of Smiles

UNIT 7

比較級

タイは、「微笑みの国」で笑顔の人々が多いと言われており、国民の9割以上が仏教徒である。首都はバンコクで急速に発展している。観光業も盛んで、商業施設やビーチリゾート、山岳地帯など、さまざまな楽しみ方ができる。また、美食の宝庫でもあり、酸味・甘味・辛味が効いた料理は世界中で愛されている。

1 Vocabulary

英語に対応する日本語を選びましょう。

1. impression (　　)　　2. confuse (　　)　　3. rude (　　)
4. benefit (　　)　　5. behavior (　　)

[a] 利益　　[b] ふるまい　　[c] 混乱させる　　[d] 印象　　[e] 無礼な

2 Word Mapping

マッピングの空所に合う語句を記入し確認しましょう。

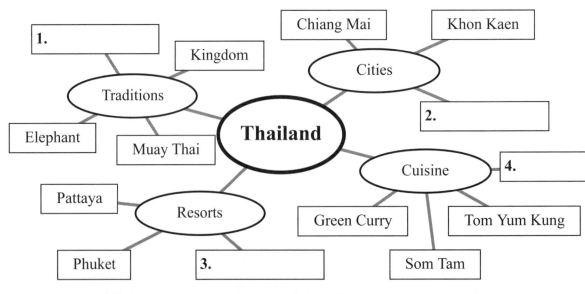

Pad Thai / Buddhism / Phi Phi Lei / Bangkok

46

UNIT 7 **Thailand** •The Land of Smiles

🌐3 Target Grammar

解説を読み文法を学習しましょう。

比較級

同じタイプの 2 つのものを比べる表現です。形容詞（副詞）に "er" を付けた形が使われます。

(1) 比較級

一般的な語	high → higher	young → younger
語尾が e	nice → nicer	wise → wiser
語尾が y	busy → busier	early → earlier
短母音 + 子音	big → bigger	thin → thinner

(2) 長い語 more difficult, more interesting, etc.

(3) 不規則変化 good → better → best   little → less → least

(4) 変化のない語 favorite, main, perfect, enough, very, etc.

(5) A は B より□： A is □ er than B/ than SV

James is younger than Paul.　ジェームズはポールよりも若いです。

He runs faster than I do.　彼は私よりも速く走ります。　◆ fast: 速く（副詞）

(6) A は ずっと□： A is much □ er than B

He is much quieter than his sister.　彼は彼の妹よりずっと静かです。

My father's guitar is much more valuable than mine.
　父のギターは私のよりずっと価値があります。

(7) A は B と同じくらい□： A is as □ as B

Ms. Brown is as old as my grandmother.　ブラウンさんは祖母と同じくらいの年齢です。

The movie is as interesting as the original novel.
　その映画は原作小説と同じくらい面白いです。

(8) A は B の〇倍□： A is 〇 times as □ as B

His new computer is twice as fast as mine.
　彼の新しいコンピュータは私のものの 2 倍速いです。

The stadium is three times as large as the arena.
　そのスタジアムはアリーナの 3 倍大きいです。

(9) すればするほど□： The more SV, the more □ SV

The more he practices, the more skilled he becomes.
　彼は練習すればするほど、もっと上手くなります。

The more we exercise, the more relaxed we get.
　私たちは運動すればするほど、もっとリラックスします。

(10) 副詞（-ly で終わる副詞の前には more を置く）

She eats more slowly to enjoy her meal.　彼女は食事を楽しむために、よりゆっくり食べます。

Nick speaks more clearly than before.　ニックは以前よりもハッキリと話します。

47

🌐4 Completing Sentences

選択肢を用いて日本語に沿った文を完成させましょう。

1. A smile is more _____ than jewelry.
   笑顔は宝石よりも貴重です。

2. Tokyo Skytree is _____ than Tokyo Tower.
   東京スカイツリーは東京タワーよりも高いです。

3. Her drawing is much _____ than mine.
   彼女の絵は私のよりずっと上手です。

4. The more we study, the _____ we get.
   私たちは勉強すればするほど、賢くなります。

5. The new edition of the book is twice as _____ as the old one.
   新版の本は旧版の2倍の厚さです。

> better
> thick
> smarter
> precious
> taller

🌐5 Word Order

語順を並び替え文を完成させましょう。

1. Mr. Gilbert _____ father.

   > than / may / my / older / be

2. The city is _____ on weekdays.

   > on / busier / weekends / much / than

3. This _____ the one I watched last month.

   > is / interesting / than / more / movie

4. The new smartphone _____ the old model.

   > as / twice / is / expensive / as

5. The more we _____ feel.

   > the / practice, / we / confident / more

UNIT 7　Thailand ●The Land of Smiles

 **Reading Trivia** 20

❶ トリビアを読み内容を理解しましょう。

The Land of Smiles

Thailand is often called the "land of smiles." Many believe this is because of its unique educational policy. From a young age, children learn never to get angry with others. This leads to people smiling and displaying the warmth of their personality. <u>The more</u> they smile, <u>the happier</u> they feel.

According to another story, in the past, when Westerners visited Thailand, most Thai people could not understand their language. As a result, their response was often a simple smile. Westerners thought their smiles were <u>nicer than</u> words, and this gave them the impression that people were happy. This led them to refer to Thailand as the Land of Smiles.

Either way, we should respect the smiles of Thai people. Being friendly to others is <u>better than</u> being rude. This policy often brings various benefits not only to Thai people but also to people worldwide.

◆ **in the past:** 過去に　◆ **as a result:** 結果として

❷ 問いに対して最も適切なものを選択しましょう。

1. How does the unique educational policy influence Thai people?
   [a] It focuses on academic skills.
   [b] It makes them competitive.
   [c] It encourages warm personalities.
   [d] It promotes challenging behavior.

2. Why did Thai people respond with a smile to Westerners in the past?
   [a] Thai people were confused by the Westerners' smiles.
   [b] Thai people found the Westerners mysterious.
   [c] Thai people smiled to show they were upset.
   [d] Thai people could not understand the Westerners' language.

3. What should we respect according to the passage?
   [a] The history of Thai people　　[b] The food of Thai people
   [c] The language of Thai people　　[d] The smiles of Thai people

49

7 Conversation with Listening

 21

❶ 会話の音声を聴きながら英語を記入し内容を理解しましょう。

> *Kosin* and *Pim*: University students in Bangkok
> Conversation while waiting in line to order at the school cafeteria

In line at the School Cafeteria

Kosin: Hello, Pim.

Pim: Hi, Kosin, how have you been?

Kosin: I have been good, thanks. What are you going to eat today?

Pim: I'm in the mood for some spicy food, so I think I will have green curry.

Kosin: To be honest, I don't like food that is too spicy, so I should choose something (1)_____ than green curry.

Pim: What do you usually eat at the school cafeteria?

Kosin: Well, I often have pad thai and fried chicken here.

Pim: Right, those dishes aren't too spicy. They must suit your tastes.

Kosin: Yes, I love them. By the way, do you know if there are any other dishes that aren't too spicy here?

Pim: In my opinion, yellow curry is milder (2)_____ green curry.

Kosin: I see, that's good.

Pim: It will taste (3)_____ milder if you top it with coconut milk.

Kosin: That sounds perfect. I will give it a try.

Pim: Please do.

Kosin: Oh, it's almost our turn. Our line is (4)_____ than the other line over there.

◆ **by the way:** ところで   ◆ **give it a try:** 試してみる

❷ 文に対して True or False を選択しましょう。

1. Pim plans to eat green curry because she likes spicy food.   True   False
2. It was Kosin's first experience eating at the cafeteria.   True   False
3. Pim thinks green curry is spicier than yellow curry.   True   False
4. Kosin finally decided to order green curry.   True   False

UNIT 7　Thailand ●The Land of Smiles

8 Presentation

❶ 発表のモデル文を読み内容を理解しましょう。

Aporn: A university student in Chiang Mai

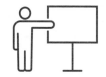

Favorite Comedian

Hello, I'm Aporn. Today I'm going to talk about my favorite comedian. Currently, I'm a fan of Mr. Silly. His style is a solo act. Every time I see him perform, I can't help laughing.

I have seen Mr. Silly a lot in the media recently since he has become more popular than ever. The number of views of his videos is constantly increasing. I watch his performances once every three days. He makes me laugh and helps relieve my stress. Indeed, the more we laugh, the happier we feel.

I enjoy his show live on TV. I hope you will enjoy his comedy as much as I do. Thank you for listening.

◆ **can't help V-ing:** Vせずにはいられない

❷ ロールプレイのため英語を記入しペア・グループ内で発表しましょう

Favorite Comedian

Hello, I'm ＿＿＿＿＿＿＿. Today I'm going to talk about my favorite comedian. Currently, I'm a fan of ＿＿＿＿＿＿＿. His/Her style is [1]＿＿＿＿＿＿＿＿＿＿＿＿. Every time I see him/her perform, I can't help laughing.

I have seen ＿＿＿＿＿＿＿＿＿＿ a lot in the media recently since he/she has become more popular than ever. The number of views of his/her videos is constantly increasing. I watch his/her performances once [2]＿＿＿＿＿＿＿＿＿＿. He/She makes me laugh and helps relieve my stress. Indeed, the more we laugh, the happier we feel.

I enjoy his/her show live on [3]＿＿＿＿＿＿＿. I hope you will enjoy his/her comedy as much as I do. Thank you for listening.

[1] a solo act, a stand-up duo, storytelling, impersonation, parody, etc.

[2] a day, every two days, every five days, a week, etc.

[3] a video site, a social site, TV, DVD, Blu-ray, radio, etc.

UNIT 8

The USA — The Gift of the Statue of Liberty

最上級

アメリカは、国際社会に最も多大な影響を及ぼす経済大国である。1776年7月4日にイギリスからの独立宣言が採択され、The United States of America（アメリカ合衆国）が誕生した。その後、様々な背景を持つ移民によって形成された国である。この多様性が技術開発と経済成長の原動力となっている。

1 Vocabulary

英語に対応する日本語を選びましょう。

1. iconic (　　)　　2. significant (　　)　　3. construct (　　)
4. vacant (　　)　　5. prepare (　　)

[a] 準備する　　[b] 象徴的な　　[c] 空の　　[d] 建設する　　[e] 意義深い

2 Word Mapping

マッピングの空所に合う語句を記入し確認しましょう。

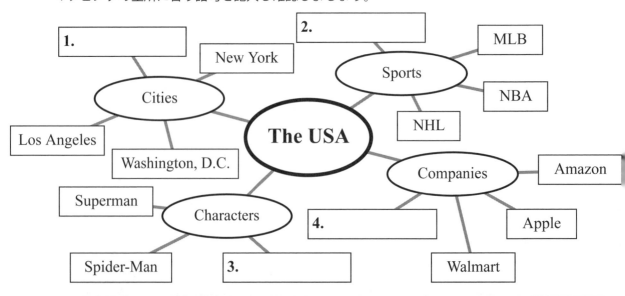

Chicago / Batman / Microsoft / NFL

UNIT 8　**The USA** • The Gift of the Statue of Liberty

🌐3 Target Grammar

解説を読み文法を学習しましょう。

最上級

最上級は、形容詞に "est" を付けた基本形で表されます。範囲の中で最も目立つ状態や程度を示す表現です。

(1) 最上級

一般的な語：	kind → kindest	smart → smartest
語尾が e：	large → largest	pure → purest
語尾が y：	easy → easiest	happy → happiest
短母音 + 子音：	hot → hottest	sad → saddest

(2) 長い語（前に most を置く）

most important, most beautiful, etc.

(3) 不規則変化

bad → worse → worst　　far → further → furthest

(4) 変化をしない語

complete, final, impossible, unique, etc.

(5) A は最も□：A is the □ est

Eagle Center is the oldest building at my university.
　イーグルセンターは大学で最も古い建物です。

Davis is the most powerful batter in the team.
　デイビスはそのチームで最も力強いバッターです。

(6) A は最も□な〇の 1 つ：A is one of the □ est 〇 s

St. Augustine in Florida is one of the oldest towns in the USA.
　フロリダのセントオーガスティンはアメリカ合衆国で最も古い町の一つです。

Paul McCartney is one of the best composers in the music industry.
　ポール・マッカートニーは音楽業界で最も優れた作曲家の一人です。

(7) 副詞（-ly で終わる副詞の前には most を置く）

My dog moves most actively in the morning.
　私の犬は朝に最も活発に動きます。

The traffic moves most slowly during rush hours.
　ラッシュアワーの間、交通は最もゆっくりと動きます。

🌐4 Completing Sentences

選択肢を用いて日本語に沿った文を完成させましょう。

1. August is the _____ month in California.
   8 月はカリフォルニアで最も暑い月です。

2. This is the _____ book I have ever read.
   これまでに読んだ中で最も厚い本です。

3. Central Park is the _____ park in Manhattan.
   セントラルパークはマンハッタンで最も大きい公園です。

4. Andy is the _____ drummer in the music school.
   アンディは音楽学校で最も腕のいいドラマーです。

5. Jane is one of the _____ painters in the art school.
   ジェーンは美術学校で最も創造的な画家の一人です。

largest
most creative
hottest
most skillful
thickest

🌐5 Word Order

語順を並び替え文を完成させましょう。

1. The _____ the city.

   the / in / tower / tallest / is

2. This _____ 30 years.

   storm / in / the / was / worst

3. Mr. Page _____ have ever met.

   is / I / person / kindest / the

4. This picture _____ all.

   of / beautiful / most / is / the

5. Olivia is _____ members of the company.

   one / motivated / of / most / the

54

 Reading Trivia

❶ トリビアを読み内容を理解しましょう。

The Gift of the Statue of Liberty

There is no doubt that the Statue of Liberty is one of the most iconic structures in the USA. However, did you know that it was originally a gift from France, and was not made in the USA?

To celebrate the 100th anniversary of American independence in 1776, a French politician proposed donating a statue as a symbol of friendship with the USA. A significant amount of funds was raised through a campaign involving French citizens.

Frederic Bartholdi designed the statue, while Gustave Eiffel handled the structural design. It was first built in France, then taken apart into many pieces and shipped to the USA on a massive ship.

Since the base was not constructed in France, the USA had to prepare it. The base is 47m high, and the statue is 46m high, so the total height is 93m. In 1886, it was the tallest structure in New York.

◆ there is no doubt that ～ : ～は間違いない

❷ 問いに対して最も適切なものを選択しましょう。

1. Why was the Statue of Liberty given to the USA?
   [a] To commemorate the founding of New York City
   [b] As a gift for the 100th anniversary of American independence
   [c] To celebrate the end of the Civil War
   [d] As a symbol of international trade

2. Who was responsible for the structural design of the Statue of Liberty?
   [a] Frederic Bartholdi   [b] Gustave Eiffel
   [c] Thomas Edison   [d] Alexander Graham Bell

3. How was the Statue of Liberty transported to the USA?
   [a] In one piece on a large ship   [b] In many pieces on an airplane
   [c] In many pieces on a massive ship   [d] In one piece on a jet

7 Conversation with Listening

❶ 会話の音声を聴きながら英語を記入し内容を理解しましょう。

Amelia and **Lucas**: University students in New York

Looking for an Apartment

Amelia: Hi, it's good to run into you.
Lucas: Hi, good to see you, too.
Amelia: The other day, you mentioned that you were looking for a place to move to. Have you found a good apartment yet?
Lucas: No, things aren't looking good. New York now has the most (1)_____ rents in America.
Amelia: You can say that again.
Lucas: I have a great part-time job. I think it pays the (2)_____ hourly wage for a student. But even with that income, it will be hard to rent a new place.
Amelia: I see. That sounds pretty tough.
Lucas: It's a problem because my deadline for moving is two weeks away.
Amelia: Well, if you like, you could share my apartment.
Lucas: Really? That's very kind of you.
Amelia: My sister and I currently live in an apartment in Queens, and one room is vacant.
Lucas: This is the (3)_____ generous offer I have ever received! Don't worry, I will pay the rent on time!
Amelia: That would be a great help for us as well! Just let me check with my sister first.
Lucas: Yes, of course. I hope today will be the (4)_____ day of my life in New York.

◆ run into ~ : ~にばったり会う   ◆ generous offer: 寛大な申し出

❷ 文に対して True [T] or False [F] を選択しましょう。

1. New York now has the lowest rents in America.　　　　　T　F
2. Lucas is currently working at a part-time job.　　　　　T　F
3. Amelia and her sister live in an apartment in Queens.　T　F
4. Lucas was accepted to share a room without her sister's opinion.　T　F

UNIT 8　The USA • The Gift of the Statue of Liberty

 25

❶ 発表のモデル文を読み内容を理解しましょう。

Dylan: *A university student in Hawaii*

My Dream Destination

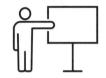

Hi, I'm Dylan. I live in Hawaii. I'd like to talk about the place I want to visit in the near future.

It's Japan. I have often seen it on TV and in magazines since I was young. For me, Japan is the most attractive country in the world. I have a strong desire to travel there. If I go, I would first want to join a sightseeing bus tour of Tokyo. I'm sure I will be fascinated by the wonderful sights there.

It takes nine hours to reach the country by airplane, so it will be an expensive trip. However, I will save money by working part-time. I'm looking forward to visiting the country. Thank you for listening.

❷ ロールプレイのため英語を記入しペア・グループ内で発表しましょう。

My Dream Destination

Hi, I'm _____. I live in _____ I'd like to talk about the place I want to visit in the near future.

It's [1] _____. This is a place I have often seen on TV and in magazines since I was young. For me, [1] _____ is the most attractive country in the world. I have a strong desire to travel there. If I go, I would first want to join a sightseeing bus tour of [2] _____. I'm sure I will be fascinated by the wonderful sights there.

It takes ____ hours to reach the country by [3] _____, so it will be an expensive trip. However, I will save money by working part-time. I'm looking forward to visiting the country. Thank you for listening.

- [1] France, Italy, Spain, England, Kenya, the USA, Australia, Malaysia, Korea, etc.
- [2] Paris, Rome, Barcelona, London, Nairobi, Chicago, Sydney, Malacca, Seoul, etc.
- [3] airplane, two connecting flights, ship, high-speed ferry, etc.

Finland *Saunas Worldwide*

UNIT 9

不定詞・動名詞

フィンランドは、国土の大半が平坦な地形で、氷河に削られて形成された湖が無数に点在する。寒冷な気候のため、都市の多くが国の南部に偏在している。人口や経済規模は小さいが、Well-being（幸福）、人権、平等が重視される社会保障の行き届いた北欧の豊かな国である。また、女性の社会進出が進み、男女同権思想が浸透している。

1 Vocabulary

英語に対応する日本語を選びましょう。

1. improve (　　)　　2. concept (　　)　　3. recognition (　　)
4. demand (　　)　　5. reduce (　　)

[a] 概念　　[b] 減らす　　[c] 向上させる　　[d] 認識　　[e] 要求

2 Word Mapping

マッピングの空所に合う語句を記入し確認しましょう。

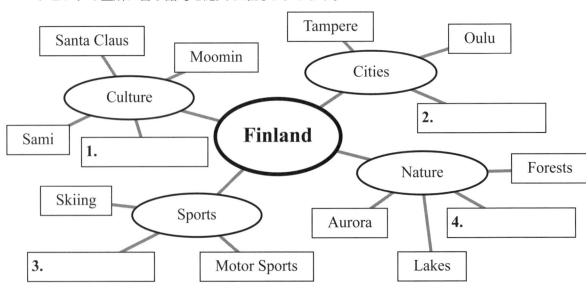

Helsinki　/　Ice Hockey　/　Sauna　/　Group of Islands

UNIT 9　**Finland** ●Saunas Worldwide

3　Target Grammar

解説を読み文法を学習しましょう。

不定詞・動名詞

不定詞は、"to V" の形で、行為の目的などを表します。
I want to swim.　泳ぎたいです。

動名詞は、"V-ing" の形で、動作自体について表します。
Swimming is good exercise.　泳ぐことはよい運動です。

不定詞

(1) 基本表現

I need to talk.　話す必要があります。

(2) 不定詞の後置修飾

Please bring me something to eat. 何か食べるものを持ってきてください。

(3) 不定詞と相性のよい動詞

"decide" の後には不定詞が使われます。
I decided to buy a guitar.　ギターを買うことを決めました。

agree to V ～することに同意する 、 expect to V ～することに期待する 、
manage to V なんとか～する 、 promise to V ～すると約束する
も同様です。

動名詞

(1) 基本表現

I like traveling.　旅行することが好きです。

(2) 動名詞と相性のよい動詞

"enjoy" の後には動名詞が使われます。
I enjoy watching movies.　映画を観ることを楽しみます。

avoid V-ing ～することを避ける 、 finish V-ing ～することを終わらせる 、
give up V-ing ～することを諦める 、 practice V-ing ～することを練習する
も同様です。

(3) 前置詞の後の動名詞

前置詞の後には動名詞が使われます。
She is good at singing.　彼女は歌が上手です。
I look forward to seeing you.　会えるのを楽しみにしています。

4 Completing Sentences

選択肢を用いて日本語に沿った文を完成させましょう。

1. I enjoy _____ table tennis every Saturday.

   毎週土曜日、卓球を楽しみます。

2. _____ manga is one of her favorite hobbies.

   マンガを描くことは彼女の趣味の一つです。

3. Emma plans _____ the piano at a local event.

   エマは地元のイベントでのピアノ演奏を計画しています。

4. We should avoid _____ the same mistake.

   私たちは同じミスをすることを避けるべきです。

5. Mr. Hill promised _____ our project.

   ヒルさんはプロジェクトを支援すると約束しました。

> to play
> making
> drawing
> to support
> playing

5 Word Order

語順を並び替え文を完成させましょう。

1. I got up early _____ dog.

   > my / morning / this / walk / to

2. _____ her own business.

   > hopes / start / mother / to / my

3. Don't _____ your English skills.

   > up / improve / to / trying / give

4. Taking _____ better.

   > feel / you / sauna / a / helps

5. We can create a _____ other.

   > by / relationship / each / stable / supporting

6 Reading Trivia

❶ トリビアを読み内容を理解しましょう。

Saunas Worldwide

Finland is the holy land of saunas. It is said that sauna culture was born in the Karelia region of Finland over 2,000 years ago. In modern times, sauna rooms gained international attention during the 1936 Berlin Olympics, when the Finnish team brought a sauna with them. Athletes from other countries took the concept back home with them. Therefore, the custom of saunas spread to many countries.

At the 1964 Tokyo Olympics, there was a high demand for saunas from athletes from various countries. As a result, sauna facilities were set up in the Olympic Village. Receiving positive reviews from the athletes, saunas gained recognition in Japan. This led to a nationwide sauna boom.

Many people in Finland consider the sauna room a sacred space, equivalent to a church, and they always make an effort to keep it clean. Today, saunas have become popular around the world. Following the Finnish approach, let's focus on keeping them clean at all times.

◆ **sacred space:** 神聖な空間　◆ **equivalent to ～:** ～と同等　◆ **at all times:** いつでも

❷ 問いに対して最も適切なものを選択しましょう。

1. In which country did saunas first gain international attention at the Olympics?
   [a] France　　[b] Germany　　[c] Finland　　[d] Japan

2. How did athletes respond to the sauna facility at the 1964 Tokyo Olympics?
   [a] With indifference　　　　[b] With confusion
   [c] With suggestions　　　　[d] With satisfaction

3. What is the Finnish approach to maintaining a sauna?
   [a] Decorating it beautifully　　[b] Keeping it cold
   [c] Keeping it clean　　　　　　[d] Using it less frequently

7 Conversation with Listening

 27

❶ 会話の音声を聴きながら英語を記入し内容を理解しましょう。

Aada and *Otto*: University students in Helsinki

Sauna Vacation

Aada: Hi, Otto. It's nice to see you.
Otto: What perfect timing! I wanted to (1)_____ to you. We are planning a trip for the next spring vacation. Why don't you join us?
Aada: Where is the destination?
Otto: We are thinking of the Lake District, specifically Tampere.
Aada: I'm not familiar with Tampere. What is it famous for?
Otto: There are lots of saunas there. As you know, we will be busy with exams before the spring vacation, so we will need to (2)_____.
Aada: So, you are suggesting that (3)_____ a sauna is a good way to reduce stress.
Otto: Exactly! In the sauna, you can enjoy loyly, which fills the room with aromatic steam and warms you up.
Aada: I see.
Otto: After the sauna, you can dive directly into the lake. What do you think?
Aada: That sounds good to me. Can I invite some of my friends?
Otto: Absolutely! All of your friends are welcome.
Aada: Thanks, I will ask them.
Otto: That's fantastic.
Aada: I will let you know when I get their availability.
Otto: We are looking forward to (4)_____ there with you.

◆ **major in ～:** ～を専攻する   ◆ **definitely:** もちろん

❷ 文に対して True [T] or False [F] を選択しましょう。

1. Aada is already familiar with Tampere and its attractions.　[T] [F]
2. Loyly helps to cool you down in the sauna.　[T] [F]
3. After the sauna, Otto suggested diving directly into the lake.　[T] [F]
4. Otto expressed concern about adding other participants to the trip.　[T] [F]

62

UNIT 9　Finland •Saunas Worldwide

 **8**　Presentation

❶ 発表のモデル文を読み内容を理解しましょう。

> *Lotta*: A university student in Tampere
>
> ### My Rules of Healthy Living
>
>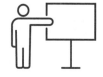
>
> Hello, I'm Lotta. Today, I'd like to introduce one of my rules for healthy living. It's taking a hot spring bath. I have been doing this for two years, usually once a week.
>
> I think taking a hot spring bath is a great way to refresh yourself, and it helps you relax. After doing that, I always find that food seems to taste better. Furthermore, my physical condition also improves. In addition, I'm able to sleep well at night. That is why I aim to maintain this routine of taking hot spring baths for as long as possible.
>
> Do you have any rules for healthy living yourself? Thank you for listening.

◆ **as long as possible:** なるべく長く

❷ ロールプレイのため英語を記入しペア・グループ内で発表しましょう。

> ### My Rules of Healthy Living
>
> Hello, I'm _____. Today, I'd like to introduce one of my rules for healthy living. It's [1] _____. I have been doing this for [2] _____, usually [3] _____.
>
> I think [1] _____ is a great way to refresh yourself, and it helps you relax. After that, I always find that the food seems to taste better. Furthermore, my physical condition also improves. In addition, I'm able to sleep well at night. That is why I aim to maintain this routine of [1] _____ for as long as possible.
>
> Do you have any rules for healthy living yourself? Thank you for listening.
>
> [1] swimming, dancing, cycling, playing tennis, exercising at the gym, jogging, going for a walk, taking a hot spring bath, etc.
>
> [2] three months, half a year, one year, three years, etc.
>
> [3] once every two days, three times a week, once a week, etc.

Belgium *The Logo of GODIVA*

UNIT 10

使役動詞

ベルギーは、首都ブリュッセルにEU（欧州連合）とNATO（北大西洋条約機構）の本部を擁し、欧州の政治的な中心地である。また、チョコレートやワッフル、ビールなどの名産地としても知られ、美しい歴史的建造物と魅力的な都市が訪れる人々を魅了する。公用語はオランダ語、フランス語、ドイツ語である。

1 Vocabulary

英語に対応する日本語を選びましょう。

1. colleague (　　)　　2. organize (　　)　　3. admire (　　)
4. luxury (　　)　　5. essential (　　)

[a] 高級な　[b] 称賛する　[c] 同僚　[d] 最も重要な　[e] 組織する

2 Word Mapping

マッピングの空所に合う語句を記入し確認しましょう。

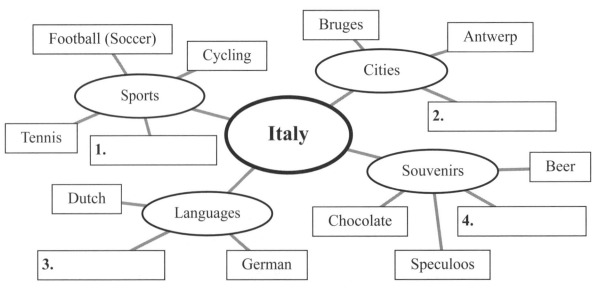

Brussels / Waffle / Field Hockey / French

UNIT 10　**Belgium** •The Logo of GODIVA

🌐3 Target Grammar

解説を読み文法を学習しましょう。

[使役動詞]

使役動詞は、人（物）に何かを「させる」という意味を表現することばです。基本形は、
主語 + 使役動詞 + 人 / 物 + 動詞の原形 です。

(1) let： S + let + 人 / 物 + V（原形）

「人／物にやりたいことをさせる」という意味です。

I will let you know when I have some information.
情報が入ったらお知らせします。

The singer lets the audience take photos at her concerts.
その歌手はコンサートで観客に写真を撮らせます。

(2) make： S + make + 人 / 物 + V（原形）

「（強制的に）〜させる」という意味です。

She makes her son clean his room.　彼女は息子に部屋を（強制的に）掃除させます。
Our boss made us work overtime.　上司は（無理やり）残業させました。

(3) have： S + have/has + 人 / 物 + V（原形）

「〜させる」および「〜してもらう」という意味です。

The coach has the players warm up before the game.
コーチは選手たちにゲーム前のウォームアップをさせます。

They had their leader organize the event.
彼らはリーダーにイベントの計画を立ててもらいました。

(4) get： S + get + 人 / 物 + to V

「〜してもらう」という意味です。

Jack gets his roommate to cook breakfast.
ジャックはルームメイトに夕食を作ってもらいます。

I got my colleague to cover my shift at work.
同僚に職場のシフトを引き受けてもらいました。

(5) 動詞の位置に過去分詞： S + make/have + 人 / 物 + 過去分詞

動詞の原形の代わりに過去分詞を使う場合もあります。

I try to make myself understood in English.　英語で理解しようとします。
I have my teeth checked every three months.　3ヵ月毎に歯を検査してもらいます。

🌐4 Completing Sentences

選択肢を用いて日本語に沿った文を完成させましょう。

1. He lets his cat _____ outside.
   彼はネコを外に出してあげます。

2. Margaret makes me _____.
   マーガレットは私を笑わせます。

3. I had my bicycle _____.
   自転車を修理してもらいました。

4. They had the chef _____ a special meal.
   彼らはシェフに特別料理を用意してもらいました。

5. She got her friend _____ the club.
   彼女は友達にクラブに入ってもらいました。

> prepare
> to join
> go
> laugh
> repaired

🌐5 Word Order

語順を並び替え文を完成させましょう。

1. Jake _____ his bed.

   > on / his / lets / sleep / dog

2. _____ the piano.

   > their / make / daughter / they / practice

3. The loud _____.

   > me / alarm / up / wake / made

4. _____ for the university pamphlet.

   > had / photos / our / taken / we

5. He _____ his decision.

   > to / got / support / mother / his

6 Reading Trivia

❶ トリビアを読み内容を理解しましょう。

The Logo of GODIVA

In 1926, a chocolate shop was founded in Brussels, and it opened a store under the name GODIVA in 1945. The GODIVA logo features an illustration of a woman riding a horse naked. This woman is modeled after Lady Godiva, who is associated with a legend from England.

In the 11th century, Coventry in England had many poor people because of high taxes. Lady Godiva, the wife of the leader of the town, asked her husband to lower the taxes to help the people. Her husband said, "If you ride naked on horseback through the town, I will lower the taxes." In response, she rode through the town on horseback, without wearing any clothes. Respecting her brave act, the people closed their windows to avoid seeing her. In the end, her brave act made her husband regret his mistake and lower the taxes.

The family of the founder of GODIVA named the company after Lady Godiva because they admired her bravery and love for the people of her city. Since then, their products have been seen worldwide as a symbol of luxury chocolate. The founder's vision let the company become known for its high-quality sweets.

◆ be associated with ～ : ～を連想させる　◆ since then: それ以降
◆ become known for ～ : ～で知られるようになる。

❷ 問いに対して最も適切なものを選択しましょう。

1. What does the GODIVA logo feature?
   [a] A store in Brussels　　　　　　[b] A bird flying in the sky
   [c] A box of chocolates　　　　　　[d] A woman riding a horse naked

2. What was the result of Lady Godiva's ride through Coventry?
   [a] Taxes were raised even higher.　[b] Her husband lowered the taxes.
   [c] Lady Godiva left the town.　　　[d] Nothing changed.

3. Why did the founder's family name their company after Lady Godiva?
   [a] Because the family was related to her.
   [b] Because it matched their original product line.
   [c] Because they admired her bravery and love.
   [d] Because it was one of their family names.

7 Conversation with Listening

❶ 会話の音声を聴きながら英語を記入し内容を理解しましょう。

Nora and Adam: University students in Brussels

Amazing Chocolate

Nora: Good morning, Adam.
Adam: Hi, have you recovered from your cold?
Nora: Yes, I came back to school today after a week off.
Adam: Welcome back! By the way, I bought some chocolate. Would you like to try some?
Nora: Oh, thank you so much.
Adam: I have heard that chocolate is good for our health. How do you like it?
Nora: The taste is amazing! It (1)_____ me feel good.
Adam: All the chocolates from the shop are delicious.
Nora: Can you tell me where the shop is?
Adam: It's a new shop next to the station. It also has a cafe.
Nora: Did you drink anything there?
Adam: I had a hot chocolate that was really tasty. I definitely recommend it.
Nora: When I was little and caught a cold, my mother used to make me (2)_____ hot chocolate.
Adam: That taste must bring back memories for you, then.
Nora: Yes, it does. Thank you for letting (3)_____ know. I think I will stop by the shop after school today.
Adam: Please (4)_____ me know what you think of the shop next time.

◆ **used to V:** よく V したものだ

❷ 文に対して True [T] or False [F] を選択しましょう。

1. Nora ate the chocolate right after Adam gave it to her. [T] [F]

2. Adam mentioned that a few chocolates from the shop are very good. [T] [F]

3. Nora's mother used to make her hot chocolate when she was sick. [T] [F]

4. Nora decides to visit the shop just before classes begin. [T] [F]

UNIT 10 Belgium •The Logo of GODIVA

8 Presentation

❶ 発表のモデル文を読み内容を理解しましょう。

Hugo: *A university student in Antwerp*

Favorite Dessert

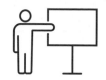

Hi, I'm Hugo. Let me tell you about my favorite dessert: waffles. They always make me happy. Whenever I see them on the menu at a cafe, I order them. They are delicious on their own, but I prefer adding whipped cream.

Also, I always drink coffee with them, which makes me feel relaxed. Sometimes, I work on my essays while enjoying them. They are essential for my studies at university. Thank you for listening.

◆ whenever ～ : ～するときはいつでも   ◆ on their/its own: そのままで

❷ ロールプレイのため英語を記入しペア・グループ内で発表しましょう。

Favorite Dessert

Hi, I'm _____. Let me tell you about my favorite dessert: [1] _____. They/It always make/makes me happy. Whenever I see them/it on the menu at a cafe, I order them/it. They/It are/is delicious on their/its own, but I prefer adding [2] _____.

Also, I always drink [3] _____ with them/it, which makes me feel relaxed. Sometimes, I work on my [4] _____ while enjoying them. They are/It is essential for my studies at university. Thank you for listening.

---

[1] crepes, waffles, pancakes, apple pie, lemon tart, cheesecake, etc.

[2] honey, maple syrup, whipped cream, yogurt, butter, nuts, etc.

[3] coffee, cafe latte, English breakfast tea, herbal tea, hot chocolate, apple juice, orange juice, lemonade, Coke, etc.

[4] assignments, projects, readings, essays, reports, research, etc.

69

UNIT 11 Kenya — The Secret of Distance Runners

仮定法

ケニアは、首都ナイロビを中心に経済発展を遂げ、豊かな自然と文化が魅力の東アフリカの大国である。サファリパークやビーチリゾートなどの観光産業にも注力している。また、40以上の民族が存在しており、カレンジン族は長距離走に優れた能力を持ち、実績のあるランナーを数多く輩出している。公用語はスワヒリ語と英語である。

1 Vocabulary

英語に対応する日本語を選びましょう。

1. oxygen (　　)
2. altitude (　　)
3. endurance (　　)
4. desire (　　)
5. acquire (　　)

[a] 標高(ひょうこう)　[b] 獲得(かくとく)する　[c] 耐久力(たいきゅうりょく)　[d] 願望(がんぼう)　[e] 酸素(さんそ)

2 Word Mapping

マッピングの空所に合う語句を記入し確認しましょう。

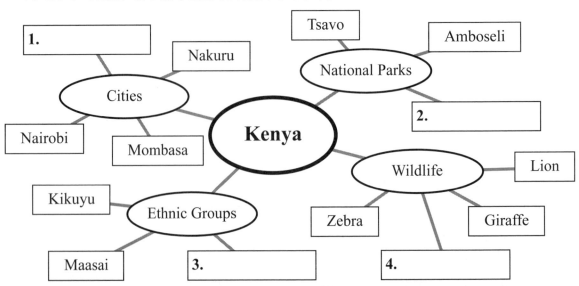

Gnu / Eldoret / Kalenjin / Maasai Mara

UNIT 11　Kenya ●The Secret of Distance Runners

 **Target Grammar**

解説を読み文法を学習しましょう。

> 仮定法

仮定法の if 節は「もし〜ならば」という仮定の意味を表し、ある事が起こるための条件などを示します。仮定法過去・仮定法過去完了では、願望や後悔を表します。主節に使われる "would" は「意図」や「結果」、"could" は「可能性」、"might" は「低い可能性」を示します。

(1) 仮定法現在（可能なこと）： `If + S + 現在形 , S + will + V`

「もし〜ならば、…だろう」

If I <u>get</u> a dog, I <u>will</u> choose a Chihuahua.　犬を飼うなら、チワワを選ぶでしょう。

If it <u>rains</u>, I <u>will</u> stay home.　雨が降るなら、家にいるでしょう。

(2) 仮定法過去（不可能なこと）： `If + S + 過去形 , S + would + V`

「もし〜ならば、…だろうに」

If I <u>had</u> enough money, I <u>would</u> travel around the world.
　　十分なお金があったなら、世界中を旅行するだろうに。

If I <u>won</u> the lottery, I <u>would</u> buy a vacation house.
　　宝くじに当たったなら、別荘を買うだろうに。

(3) 仮定法過去 be 動詞（不可能なこと）： `If + S + were + 目的語 , S + would + V`

If I <u>were</u> a bird, I <u>would</u> fly to you.
　　私が鳥だったなら、あなたのところへ飛んでいくだろうに。　◆ was の場合でも "were" を用いる

If my dog <u>were</u> a human, we <u>would</u> enjoy our meals together.
　　私の犬が人間だったなら、一緒に食事を楽しむだろうに。

(4) 仮定法過去完了（不可能だったこと）： `If + S + had + 過去分詞 , S + would have + 過去分詞`

「もし（あのとき）〜ならば、…だったろうに」

If we <u>had left</u> earlier, we <u>would have caught</u> the bus.
　　私たちが早く出発していたら、そのバスに乗れていただろうに。

If I <u>had known</u> his email address, I <u>would have asked</u> for his advice.
　　彼のメールアドレスを知っていたら、彼にアドバイスを求めていただろうに。

(5) I wish I could（不可能なこと）： `S + wish + S + could + V`

「〜だったらいいのに」

<u>I wish I could</u> own a private jet.　プライベートジェットを持てたらいいのに。

<u>I wish I were</u> a celebrity.　有名人だったらいいのに。　◆ was の場合でも "were" を用いる

🌐4 Completing Sentences

動詞を選んで日本語に沿った文を完成させましょう。

1. If we _____ the festival, we will have a good time.

   私たちが祭りに参加すれば、楽しい時間を過ごすでしょう。 (attend, attended)

2. If I _____ enough money, I will buy a new smartphone.

   十分なお金を貯めたら、新しいスマートフォンを買うでしょう。 (save, saved)

3. If Ann _____ more outgoing, she would make friends easily.

   アンがもっと社交的だったら、簡単に友達を作れるだろうに。 (was, were)

4. If we _____ closer, we could see each other more often.

   私たちがもっと近くに住んでいたら、もっと頻繁に会えるのに。 (live, lived)

5. If he _____ the earlier train, he would have arrived on time.

   彼が早めの電車に乗っていたら、時間通りに着いていただろうに。 (took, had taken)

🌐5 Word Order

語順を並び替え文を完成させましょう。

1. _____ early, I will join you for dinner.

   my / work / I / if / finish

2. If I traveled to Maasai Mara, _____.

   wild / I / lions / see / would

3. _____, she would fly freely across the sky.

   a / she / if / were / butterfly

4. _____, he would have met the deadline.

   he / faster / worked / if / had

5. I _____ the countries in the world.

   could / wish / all / visit / I

UNIT 11   Kenya • The Secret of Distance Runners

6 Reading Trivia

❶ トリビアを読み内容を理解しましょう。

The Secret of Distance Runners

Kenya is known as a marathon powerhouse. Its athletes consistently rank top in international marathon competitions. The secret lies in the existence of a fast-footed ethnic group within the country. Although the Kalenjin ethnic group makes up only about 10 percent of the total population, they have achieved significant success in international competitions, winning many medals. Most people from this ethnic group live in Eldoret, which is situated at a high altitude of above 2,000 meters. This region is known for producing elite runners who succeed internationally.

The runners live and train actively in these high-altitude conditions. Training at high altitudes is ideal for building endurance because there is less oxygen at these heights. They have a strong desire to improve their lives by earning a significant income. If they are confident in their running abilities, they will try to become top runners. Living in tough conditions makes them strong and may lead to international success.

◆ **the secret lies in** 〜：その秘密は〜にある   ◆ **be ideal for** 〜：〜に理想的である

❷ 問いに対して最も適切なものを選択しましょう。

1. How do Kenyan athletes perform in international marathon competitions?
   [a] They occasionally participate
   [b] They consistently rank at the top
   [c] They rarely win medals
   [d] They participate but do not win

2. Why is training at high altitudes considered ideal for marathon runners?
   [a] Temperatures are cooler.   [b] There is less pollution.
   [c] Oxygen levels are lower.   [d] The scenery is inspiring.

3. What motivates the runners to aim to become successful?
   [a] Fear of failure   [b] Love of running
   [c] Financial improvement   [d] Peer influence

73

7 Conversation with Listening

❶ 会話の音声を聴きながら英語を記入し内容を理解しましょう。

Sheila and **Victor**: University students in Eldoret

Marathon Runner

Sheila: Are you training hard for the marathon?
Victor: Yes, I'm in good condition. I'm about to start my run to the next town now.
Sheila: How far will you run today?
Victor: Almost 40 kilometers.
Sheila: Really? That's nearly a full marathon.
Victor: Yes, you are right. If I (1)_____ my time, I will have a chance to be selected as a marathon athlete.
Sheila: That's great. Your older brother is also a fast runner, isn't he?
Victor: Yes, he is a skilled marathon runner.
Sheila: Really? He must be very good.
Victor: Yes, but I will catch up with him soon!
Sheila: I think if you (2)_____ hard, you can reach his level. Why are you and your brother so fast?
Victor: We have always lived in the highlands, and we have been running since we were children.
Sheila: I see. What's your dream for the future?
Victor: My dream is to be a top runner. If I (3)_____ the Olympic gold medal, I (4)_____ be a millionaire!
Sheila: I think this is not an impossible dream as long as you try hard.
Victor: Thanks. It's kind of you to say so.
Sheila: Anyway, please be careful on the road when you are running.
Victor: Yes, Sheila, I will.

❷ 文に対して True [T] or False [F] を選択しましょう。

1. If Victor runs to the next town, he will cover almost 40 kilometers. T F
2. Victor started running a few months ago. T F
3. Victor's brother has been selected as a marathon coach. T F
4. Sheila believes Victor can reach his brother's level if he works hard. T F

74

UNIT 11 Kenya ●The Secret of Distance Runners

8 Presentation

❶ 発表のモデル文を読み内容を理解しましょう。

Simba: *A university student in Nairobi*

My Future Job

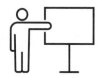

Hello, everyone, I'm Simba. Today, I'd like to share with you some jobs that I hope to do in the future. I think work is very important, so I'm thinking about it seriously.

If I have the chance, I'm considering becoming a systems engineer.

To reach my future goal, it's essential to acquire deep knowledge at university. I consider programming to be an especially important subject. I'm certain that I will study hard to achieve my dreams. Thank you for listening.

◆ consider A to be ～ : A を～だと考える

❷ ロールプレイのため英語を記入しペア・グループ内で発表しましょう。

My Future Job

Hello, everyone, I'm _____. Today, I'd like to share with you some jobs that I hope to do in the future. I think work is very important, so I'm thinking about it seriously.

If I have the chance, I'm considering becoming [1] _____.

OR

If I have the chance, I'm considering becoming an employee of [2] _____.

To reach my future goal, it's essential to acquire deep knowledge at university. I consider [3] _____ to be an especially important subject. I'm certain that I will study hard to achieve my dreams. Thank you for listening.

[1] an office worker, a banker, a consultant, a salesperson, an engineer, a public servant, a teacher, a police officer, a politician, a writer, a designer, a voice actor, a musician, a professional athlete, etc.

[2] a hotel, a travel agency, an airline company, an entertainment company, an IT company, a restaurant chain, a human resources company, an advertising agency, a car company, etc.

[3] accounting, marketing, economics, politics, tourism, education, international relations, English, engineering, etc.

UNIT 12

France — The House of Coco Chanel

関係代名詞

フランスは、世界に影響力を持つ先進国であるが、欧州の農業大国でもあり、高い農業自給率を誇っている。世界遺産や観光スポットを数多く有し、旅行者に人気の国である。モンテスキュー、ルソーといった哲学者、モネ、ゴーギャンといった芸術家の故国であり、また、ルイ・ヴィトンやシャネルなど高名なファッションブランドを擁している。

1 Vocabulary

英語に対応する日本語を選びましょう。

1. trust (　　)　　2. timeless (　　)　　3. expand (　　)
4. firm (　　)　　5. landscape (　　)

[a] 景観　　[b] 信頼する　　[c] 事務所　　[d] 拡大する　　[e] 時代を超えた

2 Word Mapping

マッピングの空所に合う語句を記入し確認しましょう。

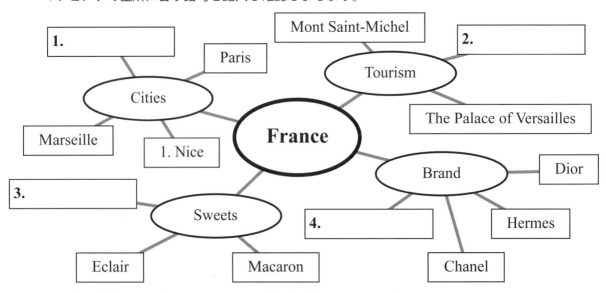

Madeleine　/　Louis Vuitton　/　Lyon　/　The Eiffel Tower

UNIT 12　France ●The House of Coco Chanel

🌐3 Target Grammar

解説を読み文法を学習しましょう。

関係代名詞

関係代名詞は、文をつなぎ、追加情報を補足します。名詞を説明するために形容詞が使われますが、形容詞だけでは説明できないこともあります。「フランス人の友達」とは簡単に言えますが、「日本文化を学ぶフランス人の友達」と伝えたい場合には、関係代名詞を用いる方法があります。

I have a French friend who studies Japanese culture.
　　日本文化を学ぶフランス人の友達がいます。

関係代名詞一覧表

先行詞	主格	所有格	目的格
人	who	whose	whom/who
人以外	which	whose	which
どちらでも	that	——	that

(1) 主格：先行詞（人）+ who の後に「動詞」がくる

I met a woman. + She sings well.　女性に会いました。+ 彼女は歌が上手です。
→ I met a woman who sings well.　歌が上手な女性に会いました。

主格の制限用法： 先行詞（人以外）+ that の後に「動詞」がくる

He has a car that seats 10 people.　彼は10人が乗れる車を持っています。

◆ 主格の制限用法で、先行詞が人以外の場合、which よりも "that" が好まれる

◆ ここでの制限とは「対象をしぼる」ということ

主格の非制限用法： 先行詞（人以外）+ コンマ which の後に「動詞」がくる

He has a car, which seats 10 people.　彼は車を持っていて、それには10人が乗れます。

◆ コンマで文が区切られ、それ以降は先行詞の補足説明となる

(2) 所有格： 先行詞 + whose の後に「先行詞に関わる人 / 物」がくる

I have a friend. + The mother is a novelist.　友達がいます。+ その母親は小説家です。
→ I have a friend whose mother is a novelist.　母親が小説家の友達がいます。
　　　　（友達の母親という関係）

(3) 目的格： 先行詞 + that などの後に「人 / 物 + 動詞（目的語なし）」がくる

This is the song. + He composed it.　これはその歌です。+ 彼がそれを作曲しました。
→ This is the song that he composed.　これは彼が作曲した歌です。

◆ He composed it. の "it"（目的語）は除かれる

◆ 目的格（that など）は省略可能　e.g. This is the song ~~that~~ he composed.

77

🌐4 Completing Sentences

関係代名詞を選んで日本語に沿った文を完成させましょう。

1. I met a singer _____ has a beautiful voice.

   美しい声を持つ歌手に会いました。　　　　　　　　　　　(who, which, whose)

2. We watched a movie, _____ is based on a true story.

   私たちは実話に基づいた映画を観ました。　　　　　　　　(who, which, whose)

3. This is all _____ I have to say at the moment.

   これが現時点で伝えたいことのすべてです。　　　　　　　(that, which, whose)

4. I have a teammate _____ father was a famous athlete.

   父親が有名スポーツ選手だったチームメイトがいます。　　(whom, which, whose)

5. Roy is the artist _____ I respect more than anyone else.

   ロイは他の誰よりも私が尊敬する芸術家です。　　　　　　(whom, which, whose)

🌐5 Word Order

語順を並び替え文を完成させましょう。

1. He _____ next door.

   the / lives / is / person / who

2. We saw _____ with children.

   that / a / played / dog / clever

3. I know _____ really unique.

   drummer / is / style / a / whose

4. I remember the _____ in Paris.

   eclair / I / delicious / that / ate

5. Stella _____ trusts at her university.

   she / friend / found / whom / a

UNIT 12   France •The House of Coco Chanel

6 Reading Trivia

❶ トリビアを読み内容を理解しましょう。

The House of Coco Chanel

Coco Chanel was a designer who influenced many people in the fashion world with her timeless designs. For a long period of her life, she lived at the luxurious Ritz Paris hotel.

Coco Chanel stayed at the Ritz Paris for 34 years, from 1937 until her death in 1971, at age 87. From her room facing the Place Vendome, she expanded her creativity in fashion and produced innovative designs. Her fashion legacy was created in the room that inspired her sense of beauty. The luxurious atmosphere of her designs continues to influence many fashion lovers and designers to this day.

What sights did Coco Chanel see from her room at the Ritz over 34 years?

◆ **innovative design:** 革新的デザイン

❷ 問いに対して最も適切なものを選択しましょう。

1. What did Coco Chanel do from her room at the Ritz Paris?
   [a] Created landscape paintings
   [b] Wrote fictional novels
   [c] Expanded her creativity in fashion
   [d] Conducted business meetings

2. Who has been influenced by Coco Chanel's luxurious fashion?
   [a] Makeup artists and makers
   [b] Event planners and firms
   [c] Architects and building companies
   [d] Fashion fans and creators

3. What role did the hotel play in Coco Chanel's life?
   [a] It was a place for socializing.
   [b] It was a temporary stop during her travels.
   [c] It was an inspiration for her sense of style.
   [d] It was a venue for her fashion shows.

7 Conversation with Listening

❶ 会話の音声を聴きながら英語を記入し内容を理解しましょう。

Henri and **Joan**: University students in Paris

Brand Store

Henri: Hello, Joan. Can you lend me a hand?
Joan: Sure. What do you need me to do?
Henri: I'd like to give Juliette a memorable gift for her 20th birthday. I wanted to ask for advice from someone (1)_____ knows her well, and you are her best friend.
Joan: Hmm, fashion is very important to her, so maybe something from a well-known brand would be a good idea.
Henri: Actually, I'm not familiar with fashion trends. Do you know the brands (2)_____ she likes?
Joan: Well, I know she loves Parisian brands. By the way, what's your budget for the present?
Henri: I plan to spend around 300 euros.
Joan: In that case, how about a bag or some accessories? I think you can find something at a brand store on the Champs Elysees.
Henri: I have never been inside a high-end brand store, but I have seen (3)_____ who are lining up outside. Are the stores always crowded like that?
Joan: No. The stores have a system where only a few people can enter at a time, so that is why they wait outside.
Henri: Really? That's surprising.
Joan: Also, it's better to dress up a bit when you go. Don't go in casual clothes like a T-shirt, (4)_____ is too informal for such stores.
Henri: Thanks for all the advice.
Joan: I hope you find something good for her.

◆ be familiar with ～ :～になじみがある　◆ be better to V: V した方がいい

❷ 文に対して True [T] or False [F] を選択しましょう。

1. Henri knows Joan and Juliette are close friends. 　T　F
2. Joan suggested buying a gift at a store on the Champs Elysees. 　T　F
3. The store allows a large number of people to enter at once. 　T　F
4. Joan advised Henri to wear casual clothes when visiting the store. 　T　F

UNIT 12　France ●The House of Coco Chanel

8 Presentation

❶ 発表のモデル文を読み内容を理解しましょう。

Sophie: *A university student in Marseille*

My Special Gift

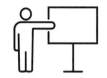

Hi, everyone. I'm Sophie. Today, I'd like to talk about a present that made me happy. The present was a smartphone that I wanted to have. It was given to me by my mother to celebrate my graduation from high school. I remember the feeling when I got it because I was really delighted.

Hopefully, when I graduate from university, I'd like to get another present. If possible, I'd love to have a ring that I have always wished for. Until then, I will study hard to complete my education here. Thank you for listening.

❷ ロールプレイのため英語を記入しペア・グループ内で発表しましょう。

My Special Gift

Hi, everyone. I'm _____. Today, I'd like to talk about a present that made me happy. The present was [1] _____ that I wanted to have. It was given to me by [2] _____ to celebrate my graduation from high school. I remember the feeling when I got it because I was really delighted.

Hopefully, when I graduate from university, I'd like to get another present. If possible, I'd love to have [1] _____ that I have always wished for. Until then, I will study hard to complete my education here. Thank you for listening.

[1] a watch, a wallet, a bag, cosmetics, clothes, shoes, a ring, a necklace, earrings, stationery, interior goods, etc.

[2] my father, my mother, my aunt, my boyfriend, one of my friends, a senior in my club, etc.

81

UNIT 13

Ireland — The Guinness Book and Beer

接続詞

アイルランドは、イギリスに属する北アイルランド以外のアイルランド島を国土としており、人口の約3割が首都ダブリン近郊に居住している。1949年にイギリスから独立し、アイルランド共和国となった。ケルト文化は広く愛され、そのユニークな音楽、伝統的な舞踏、そして魅力的なアートで知られる。また、ギネスビールの発祥地であり、パブの文化が根付いている。

1 Vocabulary

英語に対応する日本語を選びましょう。

1. publish (　　)　　2. remarkable (　　)　　3. increase (　　)
4. evaluation (　　)　　5. certification (　　)

[a] 認定　　[b] 増やす　　[c] 顕著な　　[d] 評価　　[e] 出版する

2 Word Mapping

マッピングの空所に合う語句を記入し確認しましょう。

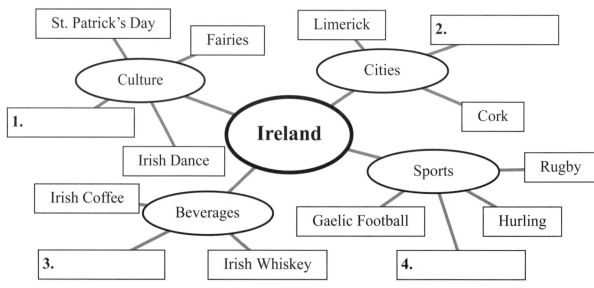

Dublin　/　Football　/　Guinness Beer　/　Pub

UNIT 13　Ireland •The Guinness Book and Beer

🌐3 Target Grammar

解説を読み文法を学習しましょう。

接続詞

接続詞は、語と語（bread and butter）、句と句（hot coffee or cold drink）、節と節（The car is old, but it runs well.）をつなぎます。英語の接続詞は「等位接続詞」と「従属接続詞」に分けられます。

(1) 等位接続詞

等位接続詞は、対等の関係にあるものをつなぐもので、 and, or, but, so などがあります。

You sing the song, and I play the guitar.　あなたは歌って、私はギターを弾きます。
I was hungry, so I ordered a steak.　お腹が空いていたので、ステーキを注文しました。
◆2つの文を and, but, or, so などでつなぐときは、前にコンマを置く

(2) 従属接続詞

従属接続詞は、メインの文（主節）と補足情報を提供する文（従属節）とをつなぐもので、 when, because, as, although, while, if などがあります。多くの場合、文の構造は「主節 + 従属節（I drink coffee when I am sleepy.）」または「従属節 + 主節（When I am sleepy, I drink coffee.）」となります。

We smile when we are happy.　私たちは幸せなときに笑います。
I was late because the bus was delayed.　バスが遅れたので、遅刻しました。
◆ because は since でも代用可能

Eric is friendly although he is a little shy.
　エリックは少しシャイですが、フレンドリーです。　　◆ although は "even though" でも代用可能

(3) as の用法

"as" の基本となる意味は、「〜のように」（e.g. She sang as an angel.）ですが、"as if" "as soon as" のように句として応用されます。

She runs as if she has springs in her legs.　彼女は足にバネがあるかのように走ります。
I will call you as soon as I reach the station.　駅に着いたらすぐに電話します。
As far as I know, Emily can speak five languages.
　私の知る限りでは、エミリーは5つの言語を話せます。
As long as you work hard, you will feel confident.
　一生懸命働けば、自信を持てるでしょう。

(4) whether の用法

「〜かどうか」という意味で、後に or not を付ける表現です。

We should ask David whether he will attend the party or not.
　私たちはデイビッドにパーティーに出席するかどうかを聞くべきです。
I have no idea whether Alice likes Guinness beer or not.
　アリスがギネスビールを好きかどうか分かりません。

83

4　Completing Sentences

選択肢を用いて日本語に沿った文を完成させましょう。

1. We will start the event _____ she arrives.
   私たちは彼女が到着次第、イベントを始めます。

2. I was sleepy _____ I was in a video conference.
   ビデオ会議中、眠かったです。

3. He acted _____ he were the king of the world.
   彼は世界の王様のようにふるまいました。

4. Dennis overslept, _____ he missed the bus.
   デニスは寝坊したので、バスに乗り遅れました。

5. I am not sure _____ she can swim or not.
   彼女が泳げるかどうか知りません。

> as if
> whether
> so
> while
> as soon as

5　Word Order

語順を並び替え文を完成させましょう。

1. _____ coffee.

> can / or / tea / choose / you

2. She _____ the exam.

> happy / is / passed / because / she

3. He works _____ tired.

> if / gets / he / as / never

4. As _____ rules, you will be fine.

> you / long / the / follow / as

5. Desmond bought _____ was expensive.

> it / diamond / although / a / ring

84

6 Reading Trivia

❶ トリビアを読み内容を理解しましょう。

The Guinness Book and Beer

Guinness, a bitter, dark beer loved worldwide, was created in Dublin in 1759 by Arthur Guinness. Also, there is a book called *Guinness World Records*. What is the relationship between the two?

The first edition of *Guinness World Records* was published in 1955. The idea initially came to the director of Guinness. During a hunting trip, he and his friends had a heated debate over which bird could fly the fastest. After endless conversations, an idea came to him. People enjoy talking about remarkable records, so if there were a book of world records, pub conversations would become more exciting, and beer sales would increase. To realize this idea, the director hired researchers and editors to publish the record book under the name "Guinness."

Today, *Guinness World Records* is known worldwide. With offices in London, New York, Beijing, Tokyo, and Dubai, official judges conduct evaluations and certifications around the world.

◆ **liven up:** 盛り上げる   ◆ **under the name** 〜 : 〜の名のもと

❷ 問いに対して最も適切なものを選択しましょう。

1. What inspired the creation of *Guinness World Records*?
   [a] A debate about birds during a hunting trip
   [b] A conversation about sports during a pub gathering
   [c] A discussion about historical figures at a dinner party
   [d] A dispute over the fastest animal at a race track

2. What was the initial purpose behind creating *Guinness World Records*?
   [a] To promote beer consumption
   [b] To settle debates in pubs
   [c] To encourage competition
   [d] To document historical achievements

3. Who conducts evaluations and certifications for *Guinness World Records*?
   [a] Local pub owners   [b] Official judges
   [c] Guinness beer drinkers   [d] Random volunteers

7 Conversation with Listening

 39

❶ 会話の音声を聴きながら英語を記入し内容を理解しましょう。

Alex and Eva: University students in Dublin

Regular Spot

Alex: Hello, good to see you. How have you been?

Eva: I have been pretty good, thanks.

Alex: Do you mind if we sit together?

Eva: Not at all, I'd like that. Here, have a seat.

Alex: Thanks. This is just my second time here.

Eva: This cafe is close to the university, and it's comfortable, (1)_____ it has become a regular spot for me.

Alex: I agree. I like this cozy atmosphere too, (2)_____ it's not too crowded.

Eva: (3)_____ the coffee is quite cheap, the quality is really high. This cappuccino is excellent.

Alex: Oh, do you like coffee?

Eva: Yes, I love it. I drink at least two cups a day.

Alex: I recently came to like coffee.

Eva: Would you like to order a coffee (4)_____ something?

Alex: Sure, I will have a latte.

Eva: Then, I will have a refill.

Alex: Let's order together.

❷ 文に対して True or False を選択しましょう。

1. Alex mentioned that this was his first visit to the cafe. True False

2. The cafe is described as never crowded. True False

3. Alex has always enjoyed coffee since he was a child. True False

4. Eva orders something different for her second coffee. True False

86

UNIT 13　Ireland ●The Guinness Book and Beer

8 Presentation

 40

❶ 発表のモデル文を読み内容を理解しましょう。

Liam: *A university student in Cork*

City or Countryside

Hello everyone, I'm Liam. Where would you like to live in the future? I believe the place where we live greatly affects our lives, so it's very important.

If we live in the countryside, the environment will be quieter and it will be less crowded. The best thing about the countryside is that the air is clean. This will reduce stress and increase our sense of well-being.

Cities, on the other hand, offer great opportunities. There are more workplaces, schools, and hospitals located close by. We can also enjoy the many facilities of urban life, such as restaurants and shops.

To sum up, although each place has its advantages, I'm now considering choosing to live in the countryside. Thank you for listening.

❷ ロールプレイのため英語を記入しペア・グループ内で発表しましょう。

City or Countryside

Hello everyone, I'm _____. Where would you like to live in the future? I believe the place where we live greatly affects our lives, so it's very important.

If we live in the countryside, the environment will be quiet and it will be less crowded. The best thing about the countryside is that [1] _____. This will reduce stress and increase our sense of well-being.

Cities, on the other hand, offer great opportunities. There are more workplaces, schools, and hospitals located close by. We can also enjoy the many facilities of urban life, such as [2] _____ and [2] _____.

To sum up, although each place has its advantages, I'm now considering choosing to live in   the countryside / the city . Thank you for listening.

[1] there is a lot of space, it's peaceful, living costs are low, people are friendly, the scenery is beautiful, we see bright stars at night, etc.

[2] cafes, bars, cinemas, theaters, concert halls, music venues, museums, shopping malls, markets, sports gyms, universities, libraries, etc.

UNIT 14

Peru — The Lost City of the Incas

前置詞

ペルーは、南米の西部に位置する共和国である。国土の西側はコスタという海岸地域で首都のリマがある。内陸部はアンデス山脈が連なる山岳地でシエラ、東側はアマゾンの熱帯雨林でセルバと呼ばれる。歴史的には、インカ帝国を含む古代文明が繁栄した重要な場所である。また、世界遺産のマチュピチュやナスカの地上絵、ワスカラン国立公園などは、国際的に有名である。

1 Vocabulary

英語に対応する日本語を選びましょう。

1. cousin (　　)　　2. cliff (　　)　　3. residential (　　)
4. preserve (　　)　　5. civilization (　　)

[a] 文明　　[b] 居住の　　[c] いとこ　　[d] 保存する　　[e] 崖

2 Word Mapping

マッピングの空所に合う語句を記入し確認しましょう。

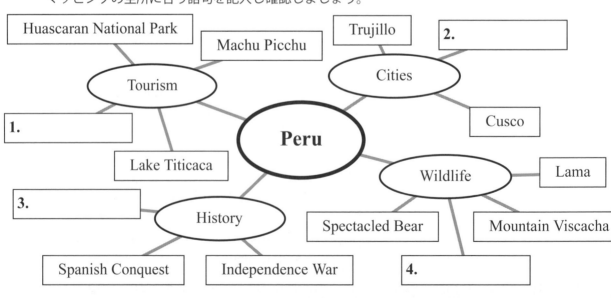

Inca Empire　/　Alpaca　/　Lima　/　Nazca Lines

3 Target Grammar

解説を読み文法を学習しましょう。

前置詞

前置詞は、名詞や代名詞の前に置くことで「場所、時間、目的」などの語句をつなぐ働きがあります。図と例文から前置詞のイメージを捉えましょう。

(1) to

対象に向かって進み到達する

I go to the library.
図書館に行きます。

We send messages to Mathew.
私たちはマシューにメッセージを送ります。

She listens to music before bed.
彼女は寝る前に音楽を聞きます。

(2) for

対象の方向を見ている

He sings love songs for her.
彼は彼女のためにラブソングを歌います。

We work for our success.
私たちは成功のために働きます。

They waited for the bus in the rain.
彼らは雨の中バスを待ちました。

(3) in

空間の中にいる

Cusco is a historic city in Peru.
クスコは歴史的な都市です。

They play soccer in the rain.
彼らは雨の中でサッカーをします。

The movie starts in 10 minutes.
その映画は 10 分後に始まります。

(4) on

ある面に接触している

The dog sleeps on the sofa.
その犬はソファの上で寝ます。

She enjoys chatting on the Internet.
彼女はインターネットでチャットを楽しみます。

We had a discussion on world history.
私たちは世界史について議論しました。

(5) at

ある一点

The musical starts at 6:00 PM.
そのミュージカルは午後6時に始まります。

My friend works at the restaurant.
友達はレストランで働いています。

We looked at the stars.
私たちは星を見上げました。

(6) from

起点から離れていく

I am from Okinawa.
沖縄出身です。

They work from 9:00 AM.
彼らは午前9時から働きます。

She is recovering from a cold.
彼女は風邪から回復しています。

(7) with

つながりがある

I study with my friend.
友達と一緒に勉強します。

She writes with a fountain pen.
彼女は万年筆で書きます。

Scott plays the piano with great skill.
スコットはとても上手にピアノを弾きます。

(8) of

全体の一部

He works as a member of the team.
彼はチームの一員として働いています。

Lima is the capital of Peru.
リマはペルーの首都です。

The city is famous for its history of a
その都市は芸術の歴史で有名です。

(9) across

横切っていく

The horse runs across the field.
その馬は草原を駆け抜けます。

Rumors spread across the world.
噂は世界中に広がります。

A rainbow appeared across the sky.
空一面に虹が現れました。

(10) over

上で行き来する

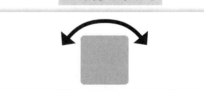

The cat jumps over the fence.
その猫はフェンスを飛び越えます。

We talk over coffee.
私たちはコーヒーを飲みながら話します。

Our project took over a year to finis
私たちのプロジェクトは1年以上かかりました。

UNIT 14 **Peru** •The Lost City of the Incas

4 Completing Sentences

前置詞を選んで日本語に沿った文を完成させましょう。

1. The university cafeteria opens _____ 8 AM. (in, on, at)
   大学のカフェは午前 8 時に開店します。

2. We cut an apple _____ a knife. (to, with, of)
   私たちはリンゴをナイフで切ります。

3. They share photos _____ the Internet. (in, on, at)
   彼らはインターネット上で写真をシェアします。

4. One _____ my cousins visited Machu Picchu. (in, on, of)
   いとこの 1 人はマチュピチュを訪れました。

5. A rainbow formed _____ the hill. (for, in, over)
   丘の上に虹ができました。

5 Word Order

語順を並び替え文を完成させましょう。

1. We _____ exam.

   for / final / hard / study / the

2. My _____ 1st.

   is / birthday / January / on / mother's

3. I will _____ classmates.

   my / play / one / with / of

4. The _____ large lake.

   flew / across / new / the / drone

5. _____ Paris on the Eurostar.

   to / traveled / Sara / from / London

91

6 Reading Trivia

❶ トリビアを読み内容を理解しましょう。

The Lost City of the Incas

Machu Picchu, a set of ruins from the time of the ancient Inca Empire, was registered as a UNESCO World Heritage Site in 1983. Many tourists from all over the world visit this place, which is veiled in mystery.

Around 400 years after the Inca era ended, Machu Picchu remained hidden from the wider world. In 1911, however, an American historian arrived there, and his research made it widely known. Located in the Andes Mountains, Machu Picchu suddenly appears on a cliff at an altitude of 2,400 meters. Temples, plazas, fields, cemeteries, waterways, and residential areas are preserved in their original state.

Why was a town built in such a remote location? Since the civilization did not have a writing system, getting to know its history is extremely difficult. As a result, many mysteries remain unsolved to this day.

◆ **be veiled in mystery:** 謎に包まれている   ◆ **remain hidden:** 隠れたままでいる
◆ **remain unsolved to this day:** 今日に至るまで未解決のままである

❷ 問いに対して最も適切なものを選択しましょう。

1. What role did the American historian play in the history of Machu Picchu?
   [a] He took people on tours as a local guide.
   [b] He started tree planting at the site.
   [c] He brought global attention through research.
   [d] He managed ticket sales for tourists.

2. What historical feature can be found at Machu Picchu?
   [a] Graveyards   [b] Theaters
   [c] Stores   [d] Hospitals

3. Why is it difficult to learn about the history of Machu Picchu?
   [a] It was intentionally hidden.
   [b] The location was not accessible.
   [c] The civilization had no writing system.
   [d] All records were destroyed in a fire.

UNIT 14 Peru • The Lost City of the Incas

7 Conversation with Listening

❶ 会話の音声を聴きながら英語を記入し内容を理解しましょう。

Paola and Miguel: University students in Lima

Tourism Report

Paola: Hi, Miguel. Which World Heritage Site in Peru will you choose for the tourism report?
Miguel: I'd like to do some research (1)_____ Huascaran National Park in the Andes Mountains.
Paola: It's the highest-altitude national park in the world, right?
Miguel: Yes, it's situated at an altitude of over 3,000 meters, and it's also home to numerous ammonite fossils.
Paola: You mean that there are fossils of marine creatures in the mountains?
Miguel: Exactly. It tells us that the Andes Mountains were once (2)_____ the bottom of the sea.
Paola: It's amazing to think about how much time has passed since then.
Miguel: I agree. What will your report be about?
Paola: I'm actually planning to study the Nazca Lines.
Miguel: Good idea. That's a very famous tourist spot as well.
Paola: It's a place filled (3)_____ mysteries, featuring geoglyphs of geometric lines and figures that look like they are extra-terrestrial.
Miguel: Is it possible to see the lines there?
Paola: Visitors can observe them from tours by plane or from an observation deck.
Miguel: Peru has plenty (4)_____ World Heritage Sites that inspire curiosity.
Paola: Yes, indeed it does.

◆ ammonite fossils: アンモナイトの化石 ◆ at an altitude of 〜: 高度〜で

❷ 文に対して True [T] or False [F] を選択しましょう。

1. Huascaran National Park is the most visited park in the world.　T　F

2. The Andes Mountains were once at the bottom of the sea.　T　F

3. The Nazca Lines can be observed only from tours by plane.　T　F

4. Miguel indicated that Peru has many interesting places.　T　F

93

8 Presentation

❶ 発表のモデル文を読み内容を理解しましょう。

Carlos: *A university student in Arequipa*

World Heritage Sites

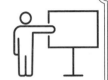

Hello, I'm Carlos. There are many World Heritage Sites, and I'd like to visit some of them.

I'm most interested in Grand Canyon National Park in the USA. If I could visit the World Heritage Site, I'd like to stay as long as possible. I think I could spend several hours there and never get bored.

While I'm there, I'd like to take lots of photos. Of course, these places are full of tourists from all over the world. I might make some friends by simply starting conversations.

In any case, I'd like to visit as many impressive places as possible. Thank you for listening.

◆ **be interested in ~** : ~に興味がある ◆ **as many ~ as possible**: できるだけ多くの~

❷ ロールプレイのため英語を記入しペア・グループ内で発表しましょう。

World Heritage Sites

Hello, I'm _____. There are many World Heritage Sites, and I'd like to visit some of them.

I'm most interested in [1] _____.
If I could visit the World Heritage Site, I'd like to stay as long as possible. I think I could spend several hours there and never get bored.

While I'm there, I'd like to [2] _____. Of course, these places are full of tourists from all over the world. I might make some friends by simply starting conversations.

In any case, I'd like to visit as many impressive places as possible. Thank you for listening.

[1] the Colosseum in Italy, Mont-Saint-Michel in France, Stonehenge in England, the Taj Mahal in India, the Great Wall of China, Angkor Wat in Cambodia, Himeji Castle in Hyogo, etc.

[2] join a guided tour, buy local crafts, purchase souvenirs, watch a sunset, create movies, sketch views, taste local food, record sounds, watch ceremonies, enter the building, etc.

TEXT PRODUCTION STAFF

edited by	編集
Taiichi Sano	佐野 泰一

cover design by	表紙デザイン
Nobuyoshi Fujino	藤野 伸芳

text design by	本文デザイン
Hiroyuki Kinouchi (ALIUS)	木野内 宏行 (アリウス)

CD PRODUCTION STAFF

narrated by	吹き込み者
Neil DeMaere (AmE)	ニール・デマル (アメリカ英語)
Karen Haedrich (AmE)	カレン・ヘドリック (アメリカ英語)

English Across the World
世界をめぐる発信型総合英語

2025年1月20日　初版発行
2025年2月15日　第2刷発行

著　　者　　佐藤 明彦
　　　　　　Richard Heselton

発 行 者　　佐野 英一郎

発 行 所　　株式会社 成 美 堂
　　　　　　〒101-0052　東京都千代田区神田小川町3-22
　　　　　　TEL 03-3291-2261　FAX 03-3293-5490
　　　　　　https://www.seibido.co.jp

印 刷・製 本　　三松堂㈱

ISBN 978-4-7919-7301-9　　　　　　　　　　　　　　Printed in Japan

・落丁・乱丁本はお取り替えします。
・本書の無断複写は、著作権上の例外を除き著作権侵害となります。